THE LAST LAP

AF378206

The Last Lap

JOHN EDDISON

KINGSWAY PUBLICATIONS
EASTBOURNE

Copyright © The Buckingham Trust

First published 1986

All rights reserved.
No part of this publication may be reproduced or
transmitted in any form or by any means, electronic
or mechanical, including photocopy, recording, or any
information storage and retrieval system, without
permission in writing from the publisher

ISBN 0 86065 414 1

Unless otherwise indicated biblical quotations are from the
Authorized version, crown copyright

GNB = Good News Bible
© American Bible Society 1976

Front cover photo: Tony Stone Photolibrary – London

Printed in Great Britain for
KINGSWAY PUBLICATIONS LTD
Lottbridge Drove, Eastbourne, E. Sussex BN23 6NT by
Cox & Wyman Ltd, Reading.
Typeset by CST, Eastbourne.

Contents

We will not weep, though summer's past
And autumn shadows fall;
These years shall be, athough the last
The loveliest of all.
                    Alfred Duff-Cooper
                    (First Viscount Norwich)

Introduction

One of the things I most enjoy watching on television is athletics, and particularly middle and long-distance running, anything, that is, between 800 and 10,000 metres. And what a lot of excitement and interest we have had in recent years! For me the most gripping moment always comes when they approach the bell, which signals the start of the last lap.

It always seems to me that this is the point where the real test begins and the real questions are answered. The pacemakers have dropped out of the race, and it is usual at this stage for there to be just three or four runners left seriously in contention. Have they trained adequately for this final challenge? Have they heeded the advice of their coaches? Have they paced themselves wisely over the earlier laps? Have they sufficient reserves of physical and mental stamina to last the course? Will they be able to produce that little extra they have never produced before, or even thought themselves capable of producing?

Long-distance running has been called the loneliest sport in the world, and you can see why. There is no caddy to consult as you stroll down the fairway, no captain to give advice between the overs, no partner to talk to at the end of a set. You are out there on your own, and failure to finish will be no one's fault but yours.

Life is a long-distance race, for some of us longer than others, and retirement and the beginning of old age is the point at which the bell goes, and launches us on the final and crucial lap. How will we finish? It will depend partly on our physical condition, of course, but also on the way we have prepared ourselves for this ultimate challenge, on our moral and spiritual stamina and on our confidence in our coach.

This book has been written in order to try to deal with some of these matters. I retired about six years ago, and am now in my seventieth year, and am therefore approaching man's allotted span of 'threescore years and ten' (Ps 90:10). So I am now in what might be called 'the back straight', not a bad vantage point from which to try to give some encouragement and advice to those who are approaching the bell.

A survivor of the famous 'few' who took part in the Battle of Britain was talking on television recently, and said this: 'A lot of people grumble about growing old, but so many are denied the privilege.' It is indeed a privilege to have been allowed to live thus far, and whatever the strains and stresses of this final lap, and the limitations and frustrations which so often accompany old age, I am determined not to complain, but to thank God for the 'unnumbered comforts on my soul his tender care bestowed'.

When I told a friend of mind about the title I had chosen for this book, he reminded me that strictly speaking retirement is not the last lap, because there is still the life of the world to come. But I am inclined to think of that as 'a lap of honour' rather than as part of the competitive race which ends with death. I think this is the sort of thing that St Paul had in mind when he wrote in his last letter: 'I have finished my course . . . henceforth there is laid up for me a crown of righteousness' (2 Tim 4:7-8). And so the best is yet to be, and the lap of honour is not just for the privileged few—the winners—but for all those who run with patience and determination, and who 'finish [their] course with joy' (Acts 20:24).

The Meaning of Old Age

A person is always startled when he seriously hears himself called an old man for the first time.

O. W. Holmes

Your old age begins,
And middle age ends,
The day your descendants
Outnumber your friends.

Ogden Nash

To be seventy years young is sometimes more cheerful and hopeful than to be forty years old.

O. W. Holmes

Every man desires to live long; but no man would be old.

Dean Swift

My glass shall not persuade me I am old.

Shakespeare

There is more felicity on the far side of baldness than young men can possibly imagine.

E. P. Smith

Give me a young man in whom there is something of the old, and an old man in whom there is something of the young; guided so, a man may grow old in body, but never in mind.

Cicero

I am your God and will take care of you until you are old and your hair is grey. I made you and will care for you; I will give you help and rescue you.

Is 46:4 (GNB)

Nothing is more beautiful than cheerfulness in old age.

Richter

1

The Meaning of Old Age

When does old age begin? It all depends! It depends on who you are, what you are and where you are. We can all remember as children imagining that the teacher, perhaps only twelve years older than we were, must have had one foot in the grave, because everyone over the age of about twenty-five looked ancient to our juvenile eyes. A friend of mine, the headmaster of a preparatory school, was once scolding the boys in his Scripture class because they seemed to know so little about Noah and his ark. 'When I was your age,' he said, 'I knew the whole story.' A hand went up at the back of the classroom.

'Yes, boy, what is it?'

'Please, Sir, it was so much nearer your time than ours.'

And I remember rather tactlessly trying to illustrate this point to a friend of mine, at that time only in his fifties, by telling him of a boy who had asked me 'who that old man was'. He was understandably not at all amused.

When I was about eight, and my younger brother five-and-a-half, I pointed out one day in a lordly manner that I was two-and-a-half years older than he.

'I shall soon catch you up,' was his reply.

I told him that this would be impossible, but of course in one sense he was quite right. At that time his age was 69% of my own, while now it is more like 96%. The difference has practically vanished; and that of course explains why the giants of our childhood seem to shrink in stature, and we wonder why we ever held them in such awe. Our idea of old age will therefore depend very much on the standpoint from which we view it, and as a sexagenarian, seventy looks to be little more than a foothill, and nothing like the almost unassailable peak it appeared to be at twenty.

Old age will also depend upon what you are. The athlete will feel that he is 'over the hill' at a much earlier age than the academic. The Olympic swimmer, for instance, will probably reach his peak before he is twenty, the footballer before he is thirty and the golfer before he is forty. I can remember the disappointment with which my father, at one time a scratch golfer, watched his handicap rise and his form slip as he made his way through the fifties; though he retained his skill as a chess-player for a good while longer.

Psychologists would probably tell us that there is also an age, though we may not be conscious of it at the time, when our mental powers begin to slow down. We find it harder to grasp the essential points of an argument. We need a little longer to find the right word. Names and facts do not come so readily to mind. As a young man I was ashamed of myself if, at the end of a camp or house party lasting nine or ten days, I did not know the names of all sixty boys who had been there. By the time I reached the age of sixty-four, I am afraid it was a very different story. To some extent this deterioration is masked and offset by the fact that we go on assimilating fresh knowledge, though perhaps at an increasingly slow rate, all through our lives. Mentally, therefore, it is very often only the onset of genuine senile decay that alerts others, and eventually ourselves, that we really are growing old.

Of course old age will depend to some extent on where we live and during which period of history. In some countries, for example, people seem to grow old more quickly than in others, and we probably know of people who have returned from the far east, or from the tropics, who look much older than they really are. And when it comes to history, of course, the average age to which people live has doubled in the last hundred years.

This is due to two things: the enormous reduction of infant mortality and the almost total elimination of so many diseases like typhoid and tuberculosis which carried people off prematurely in the last century. Pneumonia used to be known as 'the old man's friend', because it meant a comparatively painless death at an age when less pleasant methods of departure were to be expected. The apparent prevalence of cancer and heart complaints is largely due to the fact that so many other diseases have been eradicated. A hundred years ago they did not get the same chance to attack people as they do today. Other mortal diseases claimed their victims first.

So the definition of old age will change with geography and history. I remember when I was just twenty-one getting a letter from a Latin scholar who was a friend of mine, complaining that now he was forty-two he had to describe himself as *senex* (an old man). Perhaps the Romans did think of themselves as senile at that early age—an idea which is laughable in this country today.

By the end of this century we in Great Britain are going to be a nation of 'Senior Citizens', to use the horrible euphemism which is now applied to us. If the shape of society today is like a pyramid, with the elderly at the apex, by the year A.D. 2000 it will be more like a cylinder, or even an inverted pyramid.

The Foundation for Age Research has come up with some startling figures. In the seventy-five years from 1950-2025 the total world population will have trebled, and the United Nations Organization predicts that in the same period the number of over-sixties will show a fivefold increase, and the over-eighties will increase to seven times their present number. The United Nations Assembly on Ageing in 1982 stressed that the world has, therefore, a limited time in which to establish the old as a resource rather than a burden.

At whatever point we like to think of old age as beginning, it is clear that in the next fifty years an increasing number of people are going to earn that description, and a careful study of its problem and possibilities is therefore no longer simply desirable, but a matter of urgent importance.

In a fascinating lecture recently given by Derek Wigram, formerly headmaster of Monkton Combe

School, and entitled 'The Adventure of Retirement', he suggests that there are six clearly-defined stages in life: there is the pre-natal existence in the womb, childhood, adolescence, adulthood, old age and the after-life. In each case the frontier is crossed by a kind of 'death' and 'rebirth', and each stage is a preparation for the next one to come. Most people, he says, if asked to draw a graph of life, would draw it in the shape of a curve, reaching a peak at some stage in adulthood, and then declining through old age to death. But the Christian's graph would be in the form of a straight line, moving upwards the whole time, and reaching its peak beyond death, in the life which is to come.

It is for this very good reason that he dislikes the word 'retirement', which has a negative and melancholy sound about it. We retire hurt at cricket, and in military parlance it is often the polite word for 'retreat'.

I was pleased that when the time came for me to leave my job a few years ago, people wrote to me about 'refirement' and even 'retyrement', both of which seemed more appropriate to the occasion.

The French have a saying, *'Recouler pour mieux sauter,'* meaning a tactical withdrawal to prepare for a successful attack, and this seems to be the Christian way of regarding old age, and immediately invests retirement so-called with a new significance and a new importance. It is something for which adulthood should be preparing us and something which is itself a preparation for the after-life. It is not meant to be an isolated period of slow and steady decay, but a time of mental, emotional and spiritual growth. It is an overture rather than a finale.

Physically, we may soon be 'past it'. Mentally, the day may come when we have to admit that we are 'not what we were', though to the very end we may remain open to fresh news and fresh knowledge. But it is emotionally and spiritually that I believe we should be able to go on maturing and developing to our dying day.

When I speak of 'emotion', I am not thinking of passion. Indeed, one of the characteristics of old age is the cooling of passion—not that feelings are less strongly held, but rather that they are more slowly and gently expressed. Vita Sackville-West wrote a charming little book called *All Passion Spent*. It tells the story of an elderly man and woman who came to know each other in old age, how their friendship ripened and deepened, how much they valued each other, and what they meant to each other in a relationship free from passion and desire.

No, I am thinking rather of that growing appreciation of what is beautiful, lovely and of good report in history, in nature, in art, music and literature, and in the lives of our fellow men and women. The hectic involvement with life, which is the inescapable experience of us all until we retire, sometimes blinds us to the beauty of what is passing by. We are standing too close to it. We haven't time to take it in. Old age gives us the chance to become spectators once again, as we were in childhood, and it is often the spectator who sees most of the game, and who can distinguish the wood from the trees. I think it is very often this quiet, tranquil and perhaps unconscious absorption of beauty which accounts at least partly for the mellowing we so often notice in the elderly. The sharp outlines are softened. People and situations no longer appear quite so starkly black or white. The humour is a little kinder, and the hitherto slightly charmless manner assumes a new gentleness.

The other area in which there should be no change (except for the better) and decay is of course the spiritual. As Christians we should go on maturing until our very last breath, and there should be no failing of our spiritual powers, but rather the reverse—as so many of our hymns remind us. I remember a distinguished Christian I once knew put it like this, when he was asked what it felt like to be growing old. He thought for a moment, and then he said, 'Well, it's rather like being in the sixth form at school. The work is harder, but you see more of the headmaster.'

To be a rounded personality everyone needs three things: recreation, occupation and education. It is interesting to note that it is precisely these three things which, in the spiritual sphere, Christ offers us in his famous invitation at the end of Matthew 11. The 'recreation' is the presence of Christ ('I will give you rest'); the 'occupation' is the service of Christ ('take my yoke upon you'); and the 'education' is the knowledge of Christ ('learn of me'). Spritually speaking, we never leave school. We are learners to the end of our lives. I can remember the pleasure and pride with which, in 1935 (the year driving tests were introduced), I was allowed to take the letter 'L' off my car, and was allowed out unaccompanied. In the Christian life we never get to that point. We can never say we have 'arrived'.

I have ceased to be surprised, but I am often shamed, by the way in which very elderly people, Christian men and women, seem to be so ready for death, and almost welcome its quiet approach. It is not that they have not enjoyed life, or are weary of it, but rather that in their closing years they have been given a glimpse of heaven, and of Christ himself. Their 'eyes have sight of that immortal sea', and they are not afraid. It is as though one by one the ropes which anchored them to this life are loosened, and that as the time of their departure draws near, they think of death as a horizon beyond which they pass into a fuller life, into the immediate presence of Christ, and not as a precipice over which they fall into darkness and oblivion. John Wesley was acquainted with this fact, and made his famous remark: 'Our people die well.'

Such serene and steadfast faith comes, I believe, to those who take advantage of those closing years when to some extent at least 'the busy world is hushed, the fever of life over, and their work done'. They use them to come to know the Lord better. It is interesting that John, when writing his first epistle, had a message for 'little children', for 'young men' and for those he called 'fathers'. He was of course thinking in spiritual and not physical terms—of those who were beginners in the Christian life, of those growing up into maturity, and of those who had grown grey in the service of their Master; and to each he had a special word. The children were to enjoy forgiveness, the first and most precious gift that God offers us. The young men were to experience strength in their fight against the world, the flesh and the devil. But for the elderly it was the knowledge of Christ, for it was their special privilege to 'see more of the headmaster', and to get to know him better (1 Jn 2:12-14). And it interesting to note that it was this same ambition, to get to know Christ better, that inspired the apostle Paul towards the end of his life; for writing to the Philippians he said, 'that I may know him, and the power of his resurrection' (Phil 3:10). Paul had already known Christ for some thirty years, ever since that famous encounter on the road to Damascus, but he realized that there were still depths of knowledge he could never fathom, and riches he could never exhaust, however long he lived.

It need not be supposed that preparation for the next life need dilute or spoil the enjoyment of this one. Indeed, I find life goes on getting better and better, and the evidence for this is the fact that it seems to accelerate all the time. As the clock on Chester Cathedral reminds us:

> When as a babe I wept, time crept;
> When as a child I talked, time walked;
> When I became a man, time ran;
> As I older grew, time flew.

We have all probably been asked at some time or other whether we would like life all over again. Sir Winston Churchill said that he would, but would want it to start at twenty and end, I think, at twenty-five; and probably most of us would want to qualify our acceptance of the offer in some way: 'Provided I could avoid the mistakes I made last time', or 'If I could leave out my school days', or something like that. But I have often wondered, if I were given the chance, at what age I would like to be allowed to live permanently. I used to think thirty-six would be my choice, not because I look back upon it as some kind of *annus mirabilis*, but simply because it has always seemed to me to be the most perfect age, when energy and experience, taken together, reach their zenith. Energy, both mental and pyhsical, has hardly begun to wane, and for some years to come should continue on a sort of plateau; while experience has ripened to the point at which our opinions are taken seriously, and no longer dismissed as youthful enthusiasms; and in most careers people at this age have reached positions of some responsibility, and if the top is not actually within reach, it is at least within sight. In many ways too, from the family point of view, it is an ideal time. The chances are that the children are still at the 'sand-castle' stage, and family holidays at the seaside are at their most enjoyable; while the awkward 'wilderness years' of adolescence are still comfortably over the horizon. With any luck too our own parents are still alive and active, and able to enjoy their grandchildren, and the family circle is as complete as it ever has been or is likely to be again.

Yes, there's a lot to be said for 'Now we're thirty-six'. And to some extent I still think so, but with nothing like the same force, because as I move through the upper sixties, I am discovering what really tremendous fun old age can be, and I am not sure that if I were given the chance, I would not opt for my present age. But I must qualify that. I am extraordinarly fortunate. I enjoy very good health and am comfortably situated. Moroever, I can continue my work as a clergyman at my own pace, and without the pressures and responsibilities which can harass younger men. Things, I fully realize, could be very different for those crippled with arthritis, struggling to make ends meet, unable to find any form of personal fulfilment, and perhaps burdened with family anxieties and responsibilities. Talk about the enjoyment of old age must sound very hollow to people labouring under those sorts of disadvantages. But granted agreeable circumstances, the early evening of life, if that is what it proves to be, can be a very special time.

As a young man I don't think I gave much serious thought to old age. Perhaps I dared not, for it took me a long time to reconcile myself to the prospect of retirement. I suspect that most young people push the idea to the back of their mind, while some fear it, and sadly, as it approaches they even try to fight against it. It is perhaps not so much old age itself that they dislike, but its symptoms. They dread the ravages of time—the telltale paunch, the furrowed face, the bald head and the grey hairs. I remember for a short time trying to use one of those patent hair lotions which claim to keep hair at its 'natural' colour. But I thought it made me look awful, and soon gave it up; and I was encouraged to do so by some splendid verses in the book of Proverbs which ought to be in every hairdressing salon or barber's shop. 'The hoary head is a crown of glory, if it be found in the way of righteousness' (Prov 15:31); and even more encouraging, 'the beauty of old men is the gray head' (Prov 20:29). I never bought another bottle of the stuff after that; and in any case, did not Jesus have something to say about our not being able to make a single hair of our head black or white?

No, I am sure the elderly must be prepared to look their age, even if they don't feel it. There is nothing sillier than to see an elderly man aping his juniors in manners, language and dress; and when we stop to think about it, it is pretty offensive too.

People of every age have their own particular culture, style and mores, and ought to feel that they can enjoy it and indulge it without their territory being invaded by elderly men and women trying desperately to appear to be younger than they really are.

Having said that, it is important to try to convince the young that we too are young at heart, that we do understand their problems and aspirations, because they have been our own, and that in one very real sense we have never quite grown up. Surely it was this that everyone loved about Winston Churchill, that peeping behind the world statesman was the mischievous schoolboy with a catapult. Nor do I discourage the young from calling me by my Christian name—I don't think it would make much difference if I tried. I am frequently addressed by people in this way when I haven't a clue who they are. It is never meant disrespectfully, and in fact you have to know people very well these days to call them by their surname.

I remember many years ago, when I was up at Cambridge, having lunch with Dr Max Warren who was to become one of the most influential Christian leaders of this century. He told me that as he got older, the more he found himself growing towards young people once again, rather than away from them. I know exactly what he meant, and I think it accounts for the remarkable rapport that we are often able to establish with the next generation but one. You see this in the widely experienced and extremely happy relationships which are often established between grandparents and their grandchildren. I think it is partly due to the fact that the very young and the very old need each other. They need us as confidants, as safety-valves, as harmless creatures who don't exist to scold or to discipline; and we need them as an antidote to cynicism, and to restore our confidence in human nature. Somehow we are able to wink at each other behind the backs of the middle-aged. They have perforce become solidly prosaic, whereas children provide the poetry of life.

> Come to me, O ye children
>   And whisper in my ear
> What the birds and the winds are saying
>   In your sunny atmosphere . . .
> You are better than all the ballads
>   That ever were sung or said,
> For you are the living poems,
>   And all the rest are dead.

No one understood this better than Lewis Carroll, and he expressed it perfectly in the little poem he wrote by way of a dedication in *Alice through the looking-glass*.

> Child of the pure unclouded brow
>   And dreaming eyes of wonder!
> Though time is fleet, and I and thou
>   Are half a life asunder,
> Thy loving smile will surely hail
>   The love-gift of a fairy-tale.
>
> I haven't seen thy sunny face,
>   Nor heard thy silver laughter;
> No thought of me will find a place
>   In thy young life's hereafter—
> Enough that now thou wilt not fail
>   To listen to my fairy-tale.

But this is a theme to which we shall return in a later chapter, when we consider the contribution which the elderly can make to society, and how they can be a 'resource' rather than a 'responsibility' and a burden.

While many may look forward to retirement, few relish the prospect of the restrictions and limitations which must accompany the onset of old age. Shakespeare has seen to that—'sans teeth, sans eyes, sans taste, sans everything'. But those who reach it in favourable circumstances, and have prepared themselves for it, are often surprised to discover what contentment and tranquillity it has in store for them after the hectic pressures of middle age, and wonder why they approached its threshold with such hesitation.

But preparation is all-important, and we shall return to this subject in a later chapter. State and occupational pensions should take care of our financial needs, but in many other ways we have to make preparation for ourselves. Some who have eagerly looked forward to the day of their retirement, are bitterly disappointed when it comes, because it does not automatically bring the happiness they were expecting.

This is because they very often misunderstand the meaning of happiness. They think of it as an end in itself, as something they will find by searching for it; but success, promotion, achievement, authority, retirement will not necessarily bring happiness. 'He won't be happy till he gets it,' ran an old advertisement for Pear's soap. We are often like that, but when we 'get it', we are sadly disappointed. 'Perhaps . . . I ought to be happy. I can only tell the truth . . . I am wearied to extinction and profoundly unhappy . . . Fortune, fashion, fame, even power, may increase happiness, but they cannot create it.' Those words might well have been spoken by Napoleon, as he watched from his lonely and miserable exile the crumbling ruins of his empire; or by Hitler, in the closing days of the Third Reich. They were actually spoken towards the end of his life by one of our own most brilliantly successful Prime Ministers, Benjamin Disraeli.

But happiness is not an end-product, it is a by-product —the by-product of activity: 'having something really worthwhile to do, using up every ounce of your energy doing it, and then looking back afterwards, and realizing that you were happy'—that is how Professor Cyril Joad once described it during a BBC Brains Trust many years ago. It is like Alice through the looking-glass. She could not understand how it was that by walking towards the Red Queen she got further and further away from her, until one of the flowers whispered to her that she must walk in the opposite direction. She started to do so, and they were quickly brought together.

We shall not automatically find happiness in retirement by dropping anchor, and allowing time to wash past us. Retirement needs to be thought about, prayed about and carefully planned. It is almost as important to know what we are going to do with our old age as it is to know what we are going to be in adulthood, and to approach it with the same degree of preparation. In that way we shall not be disappointed, and happiness will be the inevitable by-product of self-fulfilment.

We must return to this subject in greater detail, but it is important to notice in passing how this applies to the Christian. Jesus said that it was those who lose themselves in his service and in the interests of others who find life and that it is to those who seek his kingdom, that everything else, including happiness, will be added. The Christian, therefore, approaches retirement and old age with a distinct advantage, for he has this extra spiritual dimension in which he can occupy his time and his energy.

'Get lost' used to be, and perhaps still is, a very expressive teenage form of dismissal. It was a somewhat brusque and impolite way of telling someone that you had had enough of their company and did not want them around any longer. But there could be no better advice to give to those about to retire. 'Get lost' in hobbies, interests, other people and Christian service, and you may well find that old age brings 'the happiest days of your life'.

Preparing for Old Age

In a fit of rage a king sentenced his Court Jester to death, but in consideration of his long service, allowed him to choose the manner in which he would prefer to die. Instantly the Court Jester said, 'I select to die of old age.'

The man who has not already learnt to look for the meaning of his life is unlikely to be able to organize his old age in a way that will enable him to find it then.

Adolf Portmann

The first forty years of life give us the text: the next seventy supply the commentary.

Schopenhauer

Knowing when to retire. A very unpopular chairman decided to retire at the age of seventy, to everyone's relief. He was given the usual dinner, and colleagues vied with each other in translating their relief into elaborate praise. When the time came for the old man to reply, he got up and said, 'I had no idea I was held in such high esteem. It has decided me to stay on.'

Eugene Exman

There are three attitudes towards retirement: those who 'switch off' into idleness and boredom; those who 'take up' hobbies and interests to prevent boredom; and those who see and seize the chance to 'keep on' developing their personality right to the end, widening their horizons, and giving themselves ever-increasing space in which to think, read, meditate and pray.

Everything that happens in this world happens at the time God chooses . . . He has set the right time for everything . . . I know that everything God does will last for ever . . . And one thing God does is to make us fear him.

Eccles 3:1-14, GNB

2

Preparing for Old Age

Maurice Chevalier was once asked how he felt about the approach of old age. 'Well,' he said, 'I don't much like the alternative.' Most of us would probably agree. We may not relish the prospect of growing old, but surely it is greatly to be preferred to a premature departure from this life which, for all its ups and downs, is tremendous fun. I have sometimes quoted the gallant young soldier's prayer:

> . . . give me my heart's desire
> A short life in the saddle, Lord,
> Not a long one by the fire.

But in my heart of hearts I am not sure that I agree with it. There is so much to live for, that even if I were obliged to spend the rest of my life in a wheelchair, I wouldn't want to exchange such an existence for an early death.

But not everyone would agree; for just as there are students who reach adulthood, academically well trained, but 'magnificently unprepared for the long littleness of life', so there are those who reach the age of sixty-five without any sort of preparation for what they will do in retirement and old age. Indeed, for them retirement itself is a kind of mini-death from which they seem incapable of rising again. They find nothing to do, time drags heavily on their hands, their marriage comes under increasing strain, and it is not unknown for them to die prematurely of sheer boredom. They have never learnt the art of using leisure.

Increased leisure is one of the social problems which is going to face Great Britain, and indeed the whole civilized world in an acute form in the next twenty-five years, and not just the leisure that arises from unemployment; though we must remember, as Archbishop William Temple used to say, that the only difference between unemployment and leisure is money. Leisure is the time we can afford to take off, while unemployment is the time we are obliged to take off.

In the long run, unemployment is likely to fall, as world trade picks up and later phases of the technological revolution are reached. Patterns of employment are always changing. A hundred and fifty years ago, the second largest, if not the largest number of people employed in this country was in domestic service. Things are very different now, though it looks as if for some time the service industries will continue to overtake the manufacturing industries. Unemployment is certainly our most distressing and intractable social problem at this present time, though it is worth remembering that there are actually more people at work today than there ever have been. For one thing far more women are employed. Before the war it was unusual for an upper class girl to seek a job outside a very limited number of professions such as teaching or nursing, but now the reverse is true. No girl leaving school or college likes to be without a job, nor can she afford to be. But this new phenomenon tends to aggravate the tragedy of unemployment, because in some homes several members of the family may be gainfully employed, whereas in a house just down the road, they may all be out of work. There is no easy answer to this sort of problem.

But leisure is something quite different. We have already seen that by the end of this century there are going to be far more pensioners than there are today, and when we add to that the fact that more people will take early retirement, and that there will probably be shorter working weeks and longer holidays, we can see the paramount importance of using leisure in the right way. The wise man and woman will take the trouble to see that he is as equipped and trained for retirement as he was for employment. Moreover, he is likely to have more time and opportunity to do so than in the past, and he cannot begin too soon.

Denis Healey was asked recently on television what he would do if and when he gave up politics. 'Oh a million things,' was his reply, and he listed photography, painting and writing—activities which were queuing up to be enjoyed, in which he had already had some experience, but for which at present he found all too little time. It is to be hoped that before very long these things, and many others like them, will find a place in the regular school curriculum, and not be regarded as simply extramural studies. The young people of today need to be educated for leisure just as much as for work, and unless they are, retirement and old age are going to bore them to extinction. Everyone ought to cultivate a hobby or interest which will absorb at least part of their leisure time while they are employed, and thus provide an abiding activity for retirement. And if you feel you have left it too late, there are always evening classes and seminars where something useful can be learnt.

My own personal interest has for many years been gardening. I have to confess that I started more as a conscript than a volunteer, but I quickly fell in love with it, and though by no means an expert, it gives me enormous pleasure. It is an outdoor hobby in the fresh air. It varies with the seasons. It is creative, so that you can enjoy the results. And it has a kind of therapeutic effect, because when you are working with your hands, a sort of automatic pilot takes over, and the mind is free to roam and to meditate.

I know what Dorothy Francis Gurney meant when she wrote:

> The kiss of the sun for pardon,
> The song of the birds for mirth,
> One is nearer God's heart in a garden
> Than anywhere else on earth.

I can understand her feeling, and have some sympathy with it, but of course it is a half-truth, and most if not all half-truths are dangerous. To the Christian believer God is just as present in the jungle, the desert and the inner city as he is in the garden,

> For thou within no walls confined
> Inhabitest the humble mind.

It may be true to say that it is easier to think of God when one is in a garden, but that is not quite the same thing as saying that one is nearer his heart.

I always feel, too, that to some extent the gardener is co-operating with God, and helping to fulfil the first command he gave to man, to 'replenish the earth, and subdue it' (Gen 1:28). For the Christian, gardening is a physical and practical illustration of his spiritual calling in the New Testament to be a worker together with God (2 Cor 6:1), to plant and to water, and to watch God 'give the increase' (1 Cor 3:4-9).

I have always been very grateful, too, that as a small boy I learnt some of the rudiments of carpentry—how to handle a saw, chisel and plane. My efforts were appallingly crude, but they have brought well within the range of my ability some of the things which constantly need attending to in a house.

To any, therefore, who are looking for hobbies, I warmly recommend these. They are not difficult to learn to an enjoyable standard, they are not unduly expensive, and I like to think that they have a certain scriptural authority and approval about them; for was not the first Adam a gardener and the second a carpenter?

I am always glad that I was brought up in a book-lined home, and from the earliest days was encouraged to read. In fact in those far-off winter evenings, before the radio or television had invaded our homes, my mother often used to read to us for an hour or so after tea while we perhaps modelled or knitted or did our own thing quietly. I am genuinely sorry for children who have never caught the infection of books, and in some ways I would almost rather see them read trash than nothing at all, because once the art has been learned, they can always be weaned on to better things. The man who reaches retirement with no feeling for books has a yawning gap to fill.

My own particular interest is for biography—historical, political and ecclesiastical; and interest in any one particular period whets the appetite for further probing and study, so that the thing grows by what it feeds on. Books are hideously expensive, of course, but by reading the reviews in the daily papers you can decide which are worth borrowing from the local library or even buying. There is something to be said also for forming your own local 'Book Club', where perhaps six people each buy one agreed book a year, and these are then shared among the other members. This means that you can read six books each year for the price of one. It must be arranged locally, for otherwise the cost of postage would make the whole thing too expensive.

It is not good enough to say that we will 'take up' certain activities when we retire, but that we haven't time for them now. It could well be that when the time comes the inclination and the opportunity will no longer be there. We must use the forties and fifties to cultivate interests to which we can devote an increasing amount of our time when we do retire. If we fail to do this, and if we allow ourselves to be too absorbed and involved with our work, we may find that the turning point presented by retirement is too difficult to negotiate. The more demanding our work is when we are forty or fifty, indeed, the happier we are in it, the more vital it is to begin at once to prepare channels along which new interests can flow into our lives and continue to do so when the time comes to retire.

The activities we look forward to enjoying in retirement must not simply be a way of passing the time, and preserving us from boredom, but a means of continuing to develop our whole personality, giving a positive and purposeful meaning to life. It is easy for a man at the height of his career to despise leisure, or to regard it as simply a reward for industry, like the young man who told me recently that there were not enough hours in the day for the work he had to do. But this is a completely false view of things. Leisure is as necessary to us as work if we are to develop to the full the personality God has given us.

The so-called Protestant work ethic is not to be despised. There is real merit in work, and Paul himself said on one occasion that people who refuse to work should not be allowed to eat (2 Thess 3:10). Moreover, the Christian is likely to bring to his work those qualities of industry, integrity and thrift which will make him more successful than others. But he must not become a 'workaholic'. God himself rested from his labours on the seventh day, and Jesus too knew what it was to retire from the pressing attention of the crowd. 'Being' is more important in God's eyes than 'doing', and it is with 'being' rather than with 'doing' that we shall be mainly concerned when we reach retirement, and the older we grow. I get very tired of the way people say to me, 'I suppose you are as busy or even busier than ever now that you have retired.'

'Certainly not,' I reply, 'I have long since trained my thermostat to cut out at a reasonable temperature, and the one thing I don't think I have ever been guilty of all my life is overwork.'

If possible it is sensible to begin to slow down a bit for the last five years or so of our working life, to take things a little more slowly and quietly, perhaps to go on longer holidays, and to delegate what we can to others. Not to prepare ourselves in this way means that when the actual moment for retirement comes, we have to slam on the brakes too hard, and the experience can be altogether too traumatic.

The art of delegation in particular is a very important one to learn, and we have a splendid example of it in the book of Exodus. Jethro saw that his son-in-law Moses was wearing himself out, trying to do too much, and putting himself too much at the disposal of the people, when he could have trained others to take his place on a number of occasions. To his very great credit Moses, who is described somewhere as the meekest man on earth (Num 12:3) did not resent this unsolicited advice from his father-in-law, took the hint and made the necessary arrangements, to the lasting benefit of himself and the people he was leading. You can read the whole fascinating story in Exodus 18.

I always remember an occasion when I was staying at a boys' boarding school where I had been preaching; I was enjoying a fairly late breakfast with the headmaster's wife when the headmaster himself came into the dining room, having already breakfasted with the boys, looking rather worn. He must have been about sixty at the time. 'Alan,' I said, 'why don't you have a quiet breakfast in here each day with Dorothy, and let someone else look after all those horrid little boys until later in the morning when you will feel more like facing them?' It was pretty good cheek on my part, for he was years older than I, but this humble, distinguished man, who had captained Yorkshire at cricket, laughed, and I was told afterwards adopted my suggestion, to everyone's benefit. His attitude was very different from that of the well-known rector of All Souls, Langham Place in London, to whom my father was curate in 1900. Attending the parish prayer meeting just before he went off on his annual holiday, he was heard to pray, 'Oh Lord, wilt thou be rector of this parish in my absence.'

It is so easy to think of ourselves as indispensable, and that the parish, the school or the office cannot get on without us. But this attitude of mind not only cramps the style of those who are probably ripe for more responsibility, it also makes our own eventual retirement, when the time comes, that much harder. One of my jobs in life has been to act as a governor of many schools, and from time to time at council meetings the question of a sabbatical term for the headmaster crops up. Most will accept it gladly and gratefully, for their own sake and everyone else's, but every now and then a man will dig in his toes and tell us that he cannot possibly go. 'But,' I say, 'you will be surprised how well the school will get on without you, and how splendidly the staff will rise to the occasion;' and I tell the story of the headmaster on a sabbatical holiday who received a letter from his staff saying, 'We are looking forward to your return. This motion was passed by seventeen votes to sixteen, with twenty-five absentions.' I then add sugar to the pill by saying that the art of good leadership is to create a machine that will perform perfectly happily without you. There is no doubt at all that if we can learn this secret of dispensability, it will make the final break when the time for retirement comes very much less traumatic and disturbing than it would otherwise have been:

> I need not be missed if another succeeds me
>   To reap down the fields which in spring I have sown.
> He who ploughed and who sowed is not missed by the
>   reaper,
>   He is only remembered by what he has done.
> Not myself, but the truth that in life I have spoken,
>   Not myself, but the seed that in life I have sown
> Shall pass on to ages—all about me forgotten,
>   Save the truth I have spoken, the things I have done.

It is not everyone who is as fortunate as I have been in that I was allowed to recommend a successor for my work, and that my recommendation was accepted by the very enlightened and sympathetic council for whom I worked. I suppose all of us ought to keep a record, as George Müller did, of prayers offered and answered. I have never done so, but I can think of several outstanding examples, and none greater than the emergence, after years of prayer, of the right man at just the right moment to take over my work. I was required by the society I worked for, Scripture Union, to retire at sixty-five. At the age of fifty I felt almost resentful at the idea, and never thought I should want to do so. But as time went on, I realized that some of the old elasticity had gone, mental as well as physical, and in the end I was very happy to pull out nine months before I was obliged to do so, to allow my successor to take over—a man far better qualified for the rather specialized work I had been doing than I had been myself when I started nearly forty years before.

To those who find themselves in a similar position, I would say this: You cannot start too early to pray for a successor. The choice may, and probably will be, altogether outside your control, but that need not stop you from praying. We can imagine just how earnestly Moses prayed for his 'Joshua', Elijah for his 'Elisha', Paul for his 'Timothy', and so on.

I would also say this: Don't hang on too long. It is far better to retire on the early side than too late—to go while people are still saying, 'Why are you retiring?' rather than 'When are you retiring?' Of course in most professions these days there is a set date for retirement, but where this is not the case, it is well to remember that in a world where there are always likely to be more people than there are jobs, we can keep good people down, and prevent their promotion by holding on too long ourselves. History is full of examples where this sort of thing has happened in education, the church, in politics and law, in business and medicine.

It is very easy to persuade ourselves that 'for the sake of the work' we ought to stay a little longer, whereas all the time what the work is needing is a fresh hand on the tiller; and by holding on just a few months more than we should do, we can make things that much harder for our successor, for too often that final period is not one of advance, but at best one of marking time and at worst slipping back.

That old saying which was thrown at us as children when we were refused a third helping of some favourite pudding, 'You must always rise from the table with an appetite' applies equally, I believe, to this matter of our career. If we postpone retirement beyond a certain point, we make the final break when it comes that much harder, and find it more difficult to settle happily into a new pattern of life and activity. We all want as long a gap as possible between the date of actual retirement and the time when 'the years draw nigh when we shall say, "I have no pleasure in them"'.

If approached in a really positive manner, and with the right mental attitude, retirement can be one of the happiest and perhaps most useful periods of life, just as evening is sometimes the best part of the day. I remember at a farewell dinner party for a friend I was asked to propose his health, and in the course of what I said I quoted those lovely words of Alfred Duff-Cooper, first Viscount Norwich with which he dedicated his autobiography *Old men forget* to his wife, Lady Diana Duff-Cooper, and which appear on the opening page of this book:

> We will not weep, though summer's past
> And autumn shadows fall;
> These years shall be, although the last,
> The loveliest of all.

We need to remember that for no two people will retirement be exactly the same. The self-employed artist or author, for example, may never consciously retire at all. He will only become aware of the advancing tide of old age when his powers begin to fail, and he can no longer command a sale for his pictures or his books. For others, such as the civil servant, the break is instantaneous and complete. The office door closes behind him for the last time with its files full of reports, minutes and agenda never to be seen again. While others, like the clergy and some schoolteachers, who have lived in tied houses, may be able to continue their calling in some capacity or other, but are obliged to find new homes.

In this respect I belong to a fourth and perhaps uniquely fortunate group. Technically, all my life I have been what is known as an 'unbeneficed clergyman'. In other words, I have never had a 'benefice' or 'living', or occupied a vicarage or rectory, but working for a society rather than in a parish, have been able to live in my own house. This meant that when I retired, I could continue to live where I had been for the last thirty years or more, and to do much the same work that I had been doing before, as much or as little as I had time and energy for, without the pressures and responsibilities from which my age made me glad to be relieved.

However, for many people it is not as easy as that. Having decided upon the kind of things which they want to occupy them in retirement, they are then faced with the problem of where to live. Most people have to spend their working lives 'where their bread is buttered', and for many reasons want to get away from that part of the world.

My own instinct would be to get right away into really deep country, out of range of the magnetic field of a great metropolis like London, which seems to be spreading all the time. But I am afraid that for me this simply would not work. Living alone as I do, what would happen if I were taken ill? If and when the time comes when I can no longer drive a car, how would I get to the shops, the church, the local library? And so I decided to stay put, within easy walking distance of the shops and the library, and only a stone's throw from the church.

There is another fact to consider too. However appealing it may be to cut oneself off, and however much one is prepared for the isolation and loneliness this would involve, the Christian has a debt to society, and cannot regard retirement simply as a means of self-indulgence. He will, or at least he should, want to be where he is brought into frequent contact with people, and where he can continue to exercise a continuous influence for good. Indeed, this may lead him to choose the kind of place which, if he were only considering his own interests, he would not be inclined to favour.

Then again, for the Christian, there is the all-important question of the church. Sometimes you hear people complaining about the dullness or deadness of the church near which they have settled in retirement. But they have only themselves to blame. No Christian in his right mind should choose to live out of range of a really lively church, where he can worship happily and regularly, where he may enjoy Christian fellowship, and to whose welfare he can make a useful contribution. But I agree that this is not always possible, and there are exceptions. What happens, for example, if the vicar leaves, and with the newcomer all life and sparkle goes out of the church? Do we retire somewhere else? I think not. We accept the challenge. Along with other like-minded people we do all we can through our prayers and our active service to bring revival to that church. I have seen this sort of thing happen, but it could never have done so if the Christian people, whether retired or not, had deserted the sinking ship.

The Problems of Old Age—1

My life is in the yellow leaf,
The fruits and flowers of life are gone;
    The worm, the canker and the grief
Are mine alone

Lord Byron

Have you found your life distasteful?
    My life did, and does smack sweet.
Was your youth of pleasure wasteful?
    Mine I saved and hold complete.
Do your joys with age diminish?
    When mine fail me, I'll complain.
Must in death your daylight finish?
    My sun sets to rise again.

Robert Browning

What makes old age hard to bear . . . is the burden of one's memories.

Somerset Maughan

When you bury the hatchet, try very hard not to remember where you have hidden it.

There is a wicked inclination in most people to suppose an old man decayed in his intellects. If a young or middle-aged man, when leaving a company, does not recollect where he laid his hat, it is nothing; but if the same inattention is discovered in an old man, people will shrug up their shoulders and say, 'His memory is going'.

Dr Johnson

And he said unto me, My grace is sufficient for thee; for my strength is made perfect in weakness. Most gladly therefore will I rather glory in my infirmities, that the power of Christ may rest upon me.

2 Cor 12:9

The optimist proclaims that we live in the best of all possible worlds; and the pessimist fears this is true.

J. B. Cabell

3

The Problems of Old Age—1

If there is anyone under the age of about forty who is bothering to read this book, and you are spared another world war, you will have a much better chance of reaching the age of eighty than members of any previous generation. This is because within the next thirty or forty years it is more than likely that doctors will have found the answer to the few remaining diseases which are still baffling them. Indeed, such is the speed at which medical science is advancing, that in America we are told they have already discovered a cure for a disease which doesn't yet exist!

There is, however, one thing that doctors will be unable to do. They may do much to relieve its more distressing symptoms and even postpone its arrival, but they will not be able to prevent the final onset of old age. Just as Canute demonstrated to his courtiers the inability, even of kings, to stem the incoming tide, so in their inexorable way, 'with unperturbed pace', old age and ultimately death must advance upon us all, and finally engulf us; 'For all flesh is as grass, and all the glory of man as the flower of grass. The grass withereth, and the flower thereof falleth away' (1 Pet 1:24). In Old Testament days seventy years were regarded as the allotted span for the life of man, or perhaps with a great struggle, eighty (Ps 90:10). Nowadays we can probably add five or ten years to those figures, but old age, with all its attendant problems, is something we can only escape by premature death, and we must prepare ourselves to face it when it comes.

I was talking recently to the matron of an old people's home not far from here, where I quite often go to conduct Bible readings. She told me that the residents display two different attitudes towards old age. Some fight it, resenting the limitations and frustrations it brings, while others accept it, learn to live with it, and adapt themselves to its restrictions. Of course it is foolish to go out of our way to welcome old age, to meet it half way and to encourage its approach; and from time to time we meet people who do just this, and have become, as we put it, 'old before their time'. But when finally it does overtake us, it is equally foolish to fight it. In Amy Carmichael's famous phrase, 'in acceptance lieth peace'; not in resistance, nor even in resignation, but in acceptance.

To understand the particular problems which the elderly have to face, it is necessary to examine the different component parts of life as we know it, and see how each is affected by the approach of old age. There are, I suggest, five categories which cover life as a whole, and into one or another of which can be fitted everything we think or say or do. They are the phsyical, mental, moral or spiritual, social and financial; and it is under these headings that we will study the problems and perplexities of old age.

Physical

Long before the time comes to retire, probably most of us are aware of some deterioration in our physical energy, and that a little of the youthful elasticity has vanished. As a young man I used to be a very fast walker, and on occasions had to accommodate my pace to suit older companions; and I think the first intimations I had of middle age came when I found myself asking a companion if he would mind walking a little more slowly. It is rare for people to reach retirement without some part of the physical machine giving trouble, but it usually comes fairly gradually, so that we can adjust ourselves to it, and reconcile ourselves to the fact that it is likely over the years to become increasingly aggravating; and there are probably many who are old enough to recognize themselves in the pathetically vivid picture painted by the Preacher in the book of Ecclesiastes:

> So remember your creator while you are still young, before those dismal days and years come when you will say, 'I don't enjoy life.' That is when the light of the sun, the moon, and the stars will grow dim for you, and the rain clouds will never pass away. Then your arms, that have protected you, will tremble, and your legs, now strong, will grow weak. Your teeth will be too few to chew your food, and your eyes too dim to see clearly. Your ears will be deaf to the noise of the street. You will barely be able to hear the mill as it grinds or music as it plays, but even the song of a bird

will wake you from sleep. You will be afraid of high places, and walking will be dangerous. Your hair will turn white; you will hardly be able to drag yourself along, and all desire will have gone.

(Eccles 12:1–5, GNB)

Fortunately spectacles, false teeth, hearing aids, wheelchairs, escalators and so on have done much to alleviate the plight of the people described here, but the disabilities remain, and are a source of frustration and distress.

Take deafness. I believe this affliction can have an even more isolating effect upon a person than blindness, but for some reason we never seem to extend to the deaf the same degree of sympathy and understanding that we do to the blind. We make jokes about deaf people which we wouldn't think of making about the blind; and of course it has its funny side. The quite excellent daily help I used to have was almost stone deaf, and our attempts to communicate with each other always seemed to end with friendly smiles and gestures, but almost total failure. 'What a lovely morning,' I would shout at the top of my voice. 'Yes,' came the reply, 'and I hear it's up for auction.'

I think perhaps our lack of sympathy is due to the fact that the deaf are apt to irritate us in a way the blind do not. It is infuriating when we have to shout out some platitude which in the ordinary way is hardly worth uttering at all, or repeat some feeble joke which grows increasingly banal at the third stentorian attempt. But it is a most debilitating affliction, which drives people in upon themselves and cuts them off from others; and it is too big a price to pay for the one compensation it brings, insulation from the shattering noise in which so many people have to live. In fact we might well call the days in which we are living 'The Age of Noise'. I remember a consultant once telling me that we are breeding a nation of deaf people in this country today, because of the noise of the discos, road drills, aircraft and traffic. For years I have suffered from a complaint called 'tinnitus', which I think may have been induced by the telephone; at any rate I was advised by the same specialist to hold the receiver well away from my ear.

The general slowing down and stiffening which are to be expected with the advent of old age are sometimes aggravated by the onset of those complaints to which elderly 'flesh is heir to'—things like arthritis, rheumatism and lumbago. In a book I was consulting this morning, I found a letter written nearly thirty years ago by the clergyman who prepared me for confirmation. He lived to be a very old man—the only man I have ever known who had two silver weddings. As a young man he had been an Olympic runner. He wrote as follows: 'I have had rather a rough time lately in regard to health but I'm learning that at 85 "Brother Ass" is getting a bit worn out, and must ease up quite a lot.' 'Brother Ass' was the name I believe Francis of Assisi used to give to his body, the beast of burden that carried his spirit in its journey through life; and we must be prepared for it to show some signs of wear and tear as it grows older.

I always remember a talk I heard by Dick Hudson Pope, that prince of preachers to children. 'This house,' he said, indicating his body, 'is beginning to wear out. As you can see, the thatch up here is getting very thin, and some of the stone work (pointing to his teeth) is beginning to crumble. The time will come when it will no longer be fit for habitation, and they will have to put it away. But they won't put me away, not the real me, because I shall be provided with a new house.'

This is the great Christian hope, and an echo of what St Paul wrote to the Corinthians:

> For this reason we never become discouraged. Even though our physical being is gradually decaying, yet our spiritual being is renewed day after day . . . For we know that when this tent we live in—our body here on earth—is torn down, God will have a house in heaven for us to live in, a home he himself has made, which will last for ever . . . While we live in this earthly tent, we groan with a feeling of oppression; it is not that we want to get rid of our earthly body, but that we want to have the heavenly one put on over us, so that what is mortal will be transformed by life.
>
> (2 Cor 14:16-5:4, GNB)

Old people have to try to come to terms with the fact that they are no longer physically capable of doing what they used to do twenty or thirty years before. There was a time when we could play three, even four, rounds of golf in a day, cycle forty miles, preach four times, but the older you get, the more necessary it is to pace yourself and operate within your limits. A distant connection of mine by marriage used to love to go on a cycling holiday in the days when this was a novel and pleasant activity, towards the end of the last century. But he attempted it once too often and perhaps a bridge too far, and a stone on a Devonshire roadside marks the place where his heart collapsed, and he died.

What is particularly frustrating is to find that we cannot do the things we had set our hearts upon doing after retirement. The failing eyesight, for example, makes needlework increasingly difficult for an elderly woman, while the hands that looked forward to operating a camera or using a chisel and hammer are no longer as steady as they were.

Sometimes we can adapt ourselves to changed circumstances. I was taught my cricket at school by a member of that legendary Cambridge side of 1921. He won his place in it as a fast bowler, but as he grew older, he knew that he could only last as a player if he adopted a completely different style. I understand therefore that he put himself in the hands of a professional, and became a very competent off-spinner. I played with him when he must have been well into his sixties, and I can still remember the skills with which he beguiled and dismissed almost the whole opposition.

I think the thing which I am going to be most reluctant to give up, and which will be the ultimate mark of senility, is driving a car. It is extraordinary that you will never find a person who admits that he is a bad driver. He will admit to almost any other fault: 'I can't spell—never could, you know'; 'I must apologize for my awful writing'; 'I'm dreadfully untidy'; 'But there is nothing wrong with my driving.' Somehow when we get behind a wheel our pride, self-respect, judgement—even perhaps our virility—all seem to be at stake. I am as bad as any. I think I am quite a good driver, but who am I to say? One or two of my elderly friends, whom I regard as atrocious drivers, have the same good opinion of themselves. I can still remember the first trip I made into Scotland. I was staying in Carlisle with someone in his eighties, and that seemed to be the speed at which we made this hair-raising journey there and back. Rarely have I been so relieved to reach home safely.

But when the day comes to sell my last car, I hope I shall be willing and ready. Even now I don't get the joy out of long-distance motoring that once I did, and the cheap fares for old people make rail travel an attractive alternative. And when you think that before you even take the car out of the garage it has cost you perhaps £500 in tax, insurance, depreciation and loss of interest on your capital, it makes you realize how often you could go in a taxi before you were out of pocket.

Mental

I heard Lord Coggan remark recently that 'You can always tell when a person has reached old age, because he begins every sentence with the words "I remember"'; but ironically it is a deterioration of the memory which seems to be one of the first things the elderly complain about. Sometimes I think that memory is rather like a bank in which are stored our recollections. In this bank we have, so to speak, two accounts, 'a current account' and 'a deposit account'. Into the current account go those things which only need to be remembered for a fairly short time —the shopping to be done, the calls to be made, and so on; while the deposit account contains those recollections which we have collected over the years, some of which date back to infancy.

As I get older, I find that it is the current account that begins to fail. Again and again, by failing to keep a list, I have had to make a second visit to the town to get something which I forgot to buy on the first trip; and I am ashamed to say that more than once I have motored down to the town, forgotten that I have done so, and started to walk home.

On the other hand, the deposit account seems to remain reasonably unimpaired. It is as though these recollections have been written in ink, whereas the others were scribbled in pencil, and are quickly erased. Without any apparent effort we can often recall events from the distant past, while those which have taken place recently, and may be much more important, are apt to escape us altogether.

These distant recollections rarely form a continuous film, but are remembered as a series of unconnected stills. Isolated incidents stand out, leaving everything else in shadow. The picnic is remembered because someone dropped the paté sandwiches into the river; one of my visits to the Oval as a child, because Jack Hobbs gave me his autograph, and so on.

Now as we grow older, it seems to me that the current memory grows weaker and the deposit memory if anything stronger. This may have something to do with the way in which time appears to accelerate. Rushing through a railway station at a hundred miles an hour, it is impossible even to read its name, but the distant hills seem to be almost eternally present. The older we get, therefore, the greater the tendency to dwell in the past.

So memory is a very real and precious possession for the elderly, but it is one which they need to learn how to use. In his address in St Paul's Cathedral, at the Dedication of the Memorial to those who lost their lives in the Falklands War in 1982, the Archbishop of Canterbury, Dr Runcie, talked about 'managing' memory. In other words, memory is something which is under our control, and we can allow it to sweeten or embitter our lives.

This is not the same as 'forgetting'. God 'manages' his memory, but he does not forget. I remember once, when writing Bible reading notes, using the familiar cliché, 'When God forgives, he forgets.' I have heard Dr Billy Graham say the same thing, and the thought also features in the opening chapter of *This I Remember* by Oswald Sanders. But the editor quite rightly corrected me, because God cannot forget, and the Bible nowhere says that he does. What the Bible does say is 'their sins and iniquities *will I remember no more*' (Heb 8:12). To forget is to fail to remember, but God does something infinitely more gracious, he refuses to remember.

The opposite of 'remember' is not 'forget', but 'dismember'. The dying thief, one of God's poor 'dismembered' creatures prayed that he might be 're-membered'— made as God intended him to be, a member of his kingdom. What God does about our sins is to put them 'out of mind'. He amputates them from his memory. Often we use the same sort of remark to people who apologize to us for something they have done. 'Don't think about it,' we say, 'put it out of your mind'; though often we use the rather inaccurate shorthand and simply say, 'Forget it'.

I remember how my father used to love to say, 'You are not what you think you are; but what you think, you are.' And stored away in the minds of us all are memories, sweet and sour. By dwelling upon the sour memories—the unkind things we have said or done or suffered, the unsavoury truths we know about other people or even ourselves—it is very easy to develop a hard, bitter, cynical attitude. Conversely, if we allow our minds to dwell on whatever things are true, honest, just, pure, lovely and of good report, then our minds will be sweetened, and we shall reflect the beauty and the peace of God. Not long ago I visited the widow of a distinguished war-time general. Joy, humour, peace simply radiated from her; and I was left with the thought of what lovely memories she must have.

In my garden I often think of the different habits of bees and flies. I love to watch the bees crowding round the Cotoneaster in June, seeking the nectar, and dwelling on what is good and lovely; and then there is 'the murmurous haunt of flies on summer eves' which are far less discriminating in their choice of food. We ought to be like the bees in this respect, allowing our minds only to alight upon what is lovely.

Again and again the Bible lifts our minds to the things of God, and encourages us to dwell upon them. There are probably more commandments beginning with the word 'remember' than with any other, and the psalmist sums it all up for us when he says, 'Bless the Lord, O my soul, and forget not all his benefits' (Ps 103:2). The Christian therefore has an inexhaustible reservoir upon which to draw, for added to all the other good things God has given us richly to enjoy, there is his own steadfast loving kindness.

I always remember (an example of one of those isolated remarks that stuck in my mind) how my form master at school once told us that his favourite hymn was Joseph Addison's 'When all thy mercies . . .' Ever since then, and perhaps for that reason, I have never ceased to love it, and perhaps most of all that first verse:

> When all thy mercies, O my God,
> My rising soul surveys
> Transported with the view, I'm lost
> In wonder, love and praise.

I never knew him well enough to know his inner thoughts, but years later he became the guide, philosopher and friend to a great friend of mine, and I was able to understand why he loved it so much.

Of course, as we get older, memory is bound to be tinged with a certain melancholy as one by one we bid farewell to those whom we have known and loved so well. It is partly this fact, I believe, that makes very old people look forward to death because of the reunions it will bring. So many of their friends and contemporaries have died, that they feel stranded, left behind, like those who have missed a train which others have caught.

It is here that we need to cultivate a point of view other than our own, what Dr Runcie, in the sermon already referred to, calls 'the perspective of eternity, the perspective of God'. He goes on to say, 'To see with the eyes of eternity is to see all the past and all the future together in one timeless, everlasting present. God sees, now and always, those faces we can only remember.' Walking through the city of London, St Paul's Cathedral is either before me or behind me; but to someone hovering overhead in a helicopter, it is always present. So, what to us may appear to be past or future, and can only be for one fleeting moment present, is part of God's eternal 'Now', and that is why he was known as the 'I AM'.

It is this 'perspective of eternity' which for the

Christian gives to even the saddest memories some sort of silver lining. We may not be able to 'pluck from the memory a rooted sorrow', or 'Raze out the written troubles of the brain . . . with some oblivious antidote', as Macbeth asks the doctor. But his reply goes to the root of the problem when he says, 'Therein the patient must minister to himself.'

In other words, it is a matter of the will. We can, with God's help, very largely 'manage' our memories. We can refuse to entertain those that would oblige us to indulge in self-pity over some supposed slight or injury; or to wallow in someone else's misfortune; or to allow ourselves unnecessary remorse and heartache over something which God has forgiven, but which we cannot quite forgive ourselves.

There is another mental attitude which the elderly need to learn to control or manage, and that is their imagination. Like children, old people have a very vivid imagination, but it runs in a different direction. Broadly speaking, children imagine the things they could do, and like to see themselves as heroes or heroines; while the elderly imagine what they can suffer, and see themselves as the victims of insults, perhaps, or illness or even insolvency.

It is very easy for old people to imagine that they have been slighted in some way, and to take offence. It may be that they did not quite hear what was said, or that they misunderstood some comment, reading into it far more than was intended. Perhaps they cannot quite keep up with the conversation, and feel that they are gently but deliberately being pushed to one side and left out. Sometimes, of course, there is insensitivity on the part of other people, and even impatience and discourtesy. This is to be deplored, and we shall return to it later; but for their part old people must not jump to conclusions, overreact and allow their imagination to run away with them.

It is easy, too, for the elderly to imagine that there is something seriously wrong with them, when in fact their only trouble is that they are growing old. Mild hypochondria is fairly common amongst the elderly, especially if they live alone. A good friend of mind who was this way inclined rang up a doctor friend of his: 'Doctor, I had a cough which went like this (demonstration over the telephone) and you gave me some medicine for it. I now have a cough which goes like this (further demonstration) would the same medicine do?' It is only fair to add that when he did have to have two quite nasty operations when he was well into his seventies, he faced them with complete equanimity.

Then sometimes quite wealthy people can imagine that they are on the point of insolvency. Bernard Shaw, when he died in 1950, left £350,000, which today would have made him a millionaire several times over. But he was obsessed with the taxes he had to pay, and was convinced he was heading for bankruptcy. And Sheridan Morley, in his life of David Niven, tells us that he was a rich man who went to his grave convinced that he couldn't afford to pay for a nurse to look after him.

I have often pondered this curious but not unusual phenomenon. It is not that such people are ungenerous, or miserly, though perhaps miserliness is related to it. No doubt psychologists would be able to offer an explanation, but it certainly bears out what the Bible says about the dangers of trusting in the uncertainty of riches (1 Tim 6:17). It is indeed ironical if the one thing which is supposed to bring material comfort and wellbeing in old age fails at the last to do so. It was something John Bunyan understood clearly when he wrote the Shepherd Boy's Song in *Pilgrim's Progress:*

> Fulness to such a burden is
> That go on pilgrimage;
> Here little and hereafter bliss
> Is best from age to age.

Spiritual

A not dissimilar problem sometimes faces Christian people in their old age. Having lived until then what might be called 'wealthy' spiritual lives, full of faith and peace and joy, they find themselves suddenly and inexplicably plunged into darkness and doubt from which there seems to be no escape. It is a most distressing sight to see those who have been wonderfully used by God in the past floundering in the waters through which they have guided and helped scores and even hundreds of others.

I don't believe it has anything to do with the fear of death. Indeed, such people are tempted to long for death if it will put them out of their misery. Nor is it uniquely the experience of those who have suffered from depression all their lives, like the poet William Cowper who expressed the state of mind so poignantly in his hymn, 'O for a closer walk with God':

> Where is the blessedness I knew
> When first I met the Lord?
> And where the soul-refreshing view
> Of Jesus and his word?

> What peaceful hours I once enjoyed!
> How sweet their memory still!
> But they have left an aching void
> The world can never fill.

Indeed, sometimes those who have suffered from depression for many years come through at the end into much calmer waters, and into a peace of mind they have not known for years, though I do not think this was so in the experience of William Cowper.

If it is not the fear of death, and if it is not part of a long history of mental depression, then what is the cause? There may, I suppose, be a psychological or a biological explanation, but my own belief is that it is an attack of Satan. It is Satan trying to get his revenge upon someone who all his life has been a thorn in his flesh. It is his last chance, and he means to take it, for in a few years' time the person concerned will be out of his reach, in a place where 'God shall wipe away all tears from their eyes; and there shall be no more death, neither sorrow, nor crying, neither shall there be any more pain' (Rev 21:4).

The Bible is not without hints of this problem. Was David aware of it when he prayed, 'Cast me not off in the time of old age; forsake me not when my strength faileth . . . when I am old and gray-headed, O God, forsake me not' (Ps 71:9, 18)? And what about John the Baptist, as he lay languishing in prison? He too was assailed with doubt. Had he been mistaken all along? Had he built his house upon the sand? Urgently he sent his disciples to Jesus, 'Are you the one who was to come, or should we expect someone else?' I always like Jesus' answer. It was not a theological one, though of course it had tremendous theological implications; but a practical one: 'Go back and report to John what you have seen and heard . . .' (Lk 7:19-23, New International Version).

I think it may be in this sort of way that we can best help the victims of doubt and distress. They know all the doctrinal arguments by heart, and must have been over them again and again: the existence of God, the divinity of Christ, and so on. But perhaps to be told what God is still doing in the world, to learn of the fresh triumphs of his grace, may fan the flickering flame. How are we to account for such marvellous happenings if God has forsaken his world and is no longer standing by his servants?

However, I must not give the impression that this experience is more common than it is. The vast majority of Christians enjoy a peaceful old age, full of faith, and in a later chapter we shall be considering some of them. But the phenomenon is common enough for us to take it seriously, and people in this distressing condition need all the help we can give them with our advice, our sympathy and our prayers. If I am right, and it is the work of Satan, then we know that he can be overcome through the power of Christ.

I have one final thought on this subject. I believe we can forearm ourselves against this particular attack. I am always a little suspicous of Christians who claim never to have had a moment's doubt. Never even for a moment, they tell us, have they questioned the existence of God or the truth of Christianity. I used to consider such people fortunate, but now I am less sure. In common, I suspect, with most Christians I have known times of doubt and uncertainty, when my faith has been strained by creeds or by mysteries beyond my understanding.

Jesus always disintguished between unbelief and doubt. Unbelief was a refusal to take him at his word—a vote of no confidence amounting to disobedience. The issue was a moral one, and it aroused his indignation. But to those whose faith was weak, and who could not dispel their doubts, his attitude was invariably one of gentle but firm sympathy.

Doubt is a kind of growing-pain, almost a sign of progress. It is the shadow cast by faith, for just as shadows tell us that somewhere the sun is shining, so doubts tell us that dimly perhaps and intermittently, faith is at work. And it is worth remembering that even atheists have their doubts. It was Bacon who said, 'By night an atheist half believes in God.' 'What,' he must ask himself, 'what if after all there is a God?'

To live in the twilight of doubt and uncertainty of course is no one's idea of fun; but I wonder whether those who have wrestled with doubt in their earlier years, and, as it were, inoculated themselves against a major attack, are not better equipped to resist Satan's all-out assault if it comes in their closing years.

The Problems of Old Age—2

You may be old at forty and young at eighty; but you are genuinely old at any age if:

You feel old;
You feel you have learnt all there is to learn;
You find yourself saying, 'I am too old for that'.
You feel tomorrow holds no promise.
You take no interest in the activities of youth.
You would rather talk than listen.
You long for 'the good old days', feeling they were best.

Minnesota Medical Association

Pray that your loneliness may spur you into finding something to live for, great enough to die for.

Dag Hammarskjöld

When Sir Robert Walpole was dismissed from all his employments, he retired to Houghton and walked into the library. He took down a book from a shelf, held it to his eyes for some minutes, and then exchanged it for another which he held for half as long,

before taking a third, which he returned instantly,
and burst into tears. 'I have lived a life of business for
so long', he said, 'that I have lost my taste for reading,
and now—what shall I do?'

Money is like manure, it needs to be spread widely if
it is to do lasting good.

Money will buy you a beautiful dog, but only love will
make it wag its tail.

A rich banker died, and left instructions for his funeral to include the hymn, 'Guide me O thou great
Jehovah'. Unfortunately in the last verse there was a
misprint, and instead of 'Land *me* safe on Canaan's
side', it read, 'Land *my* safe . . .'

A good man leaveth an inheritance to his children's
children.

Prov 13:22

Be content with such things as ye have: for he hath
said, 'I will never leave thee, nor forsake thee.'

Heb 13:5

4
The Problems of Old Age—2

Social

One of the marks of progress within the last hundred, even fifty years, has been the tremendous help that has been mounted in support of the elderly. 'Age Concern', 'Help the Aged', 'The Foundation for Age Research' are some examples of organizations which have come into existence with the sole purpose of making the last ten or fifteen years of a person's life enjoyable, and in many cases bearable; though as Bishop Trevor Huddleston said, in a sermon preached for 'Help the Aged' in St Martin-in-the-Fields, 'that in an affluent society like ours the fact that such an effort is needed at all is a measure of our misunderstanding of human priorities'. What has happened that the elderly have become a 'problem area'? In Old Testament days it was a mark of God's blessing that people reached a 'good old age' and were 'full of years' (Gen 25:8). In Ian Hay's fine phrase, 'Old age is nature's only real aristocracy.' We have allowed it to become a burden rather than a resource.

It has to be admitted, though, that the elderly are not the easiest people in the world to help, and this for a very simple reason: they want at one and the same time two things which are radically incompatible—security and liberty. This age-old conflict is seen in every area of life. On the personal level, the child enjoys or should enjoy complete security, but its liberty is restricted; while as we move through adolescence to adulthood, and have to make our way in the world, and stand on our own feet, we enjoy liberty, but at the cost of a certain amount of security. On a national level we see the same thing in the emerging countries of the third world. One after another they have opted for the liberty of national independence in favour of the security they enjoyed under colonial rule.

In old age we tend to want both. We want the liberty we have enjoyed for so long, but we need the security we experienced as children. Complete security would mean that at the first breath of senility old people were 'institutionalized' (to use the awful modern jargon); while complete liberty would mean that they were left to fend for themselves until they were well into their eighties or even nineties. The danger of the first is boredom, soullessness and loss of individuality; while the latter could lead to undetected deprivation or sickness.

It is this sort of problem that organizations such as 'Age Concern' are very aware of and doing their best to solve. In Sheffield, for example, a 'Support System' has been developed which allows the elderly to continue to live where they are, alone if necessary, but knowing exactly where they can turn for help in time of need, while a watchful, caring and unobtrusive eye is kept on their welfare and progress. Thus men and women are encouraged to live alone, if they are obliged to do so, but know that there is a form of social scaffolding to support them.

In this way individual dignity is preserved without danger. Old people can go on living surrounded by the things that have given them pleasure in life, and not dreading the day when they must be 'put away'. But it is obvious that in largely rural areas this sort of thing would be impractical, which is why an increasing number of old people's homes are necessarily being started or enlarged. Those in charge are tackling the same problem in a different way, the liberty taking the form of individual rooms or flats, while the security is provided by the staff. I know from experience how much this is appreciated by those whose circumstances make it unwise or even impossible for them to be left on their own.

Another development is the provision of 'Granny flats', and new houses are even being built with a wing or an annexe to meet this need; for social needs are always dictating patterns of architecture, as we can see if we compare the kitchens of today with those that were built a hundred years ago. Then they looked out on to the laurels and dustbins, but now they command one of the best views in the house.

Undoubtedly one of the hardest things for old people to get used to is loneliness. It can often begin at the very moment of retirement. There is the sudden and irreversible loss of the people we have been working with for years—partners, parishioners, patients, pupils or whatever. It leaves a sense of emptiness, and perhaps that is why retirement has been described as 'a mini-death', a rehearsal for the real thing which it is to be hoped still lies some years in the future.

There is an awful sense of finality about death, so far as this world is concerned. A person dies, even a famous person whose name is a household word, and what happens? There is quiet family funeral, an obituary in *The Times,* and then after a decent interval, a Memorial or Thanksgiving Service, a tablet in the local church and perhaps a biography. But for the rest of the world life goes on just as before. What was a 'current affair' yesterday is 'history' today. The name is removed from reference books and directories, and the person concerned becomes, in Whittier's words, 'a dead fact stranded on the shore of the oblivious years'. 'And some there be which have no memorial; who are perished as though they had never been, and are become as though they had not been born' (Ecclesiasticus 44:9).

Of course retirement is not as bad as that. A man does not become a 'Never was', but only a 'Has been'; but it can be a wounding and distressing experience. You go back to the old office or place of work, and while they seem quite pleased to see you, you are no longer needed. They can get on without you, and you are made to feel a slight intruder. I don't know that it can be helped. Perhaps the amputation has to be complete, and the work has to go on. But I sometimes wish that in semi-official ways professions and firms could make more use of the wisdom and experience of past employees. I think it would be appreciated much more than the farewell party and the gold watch.

There is a second, even more inescapable cause of loneliness: the older we grow, the more friends and relations we lose through death, and it is to the obituary columns in the papers that we begin to turn first, rather than engagements, marriages, births and christenings. The centenarian is indeed to be congratulated, but we must spare a thought for him, because probably he alone is left from among his contemporaries. From time to time I visit an elderly relation of mine, now well into her eighties, but still very spry, and living in a very comforable old people's home run by the Royal United Kingdom Benevolent Association (RUKBA). My mother was her first cousin, but now she is the only survivor of that generation, and it must be a lonely experience to have to say with Elijah, 'I, even I only, am left' (1 Kings 19:10).

Loneliness can also be aggravated by what is called 'the generation gap'. It is interesting to notice, as Paul Tournier points out in his book *Learning to Grow Old*, that young people have established for themselves a separate, identifiable and clearly-defined niche in society. Fifty years ago we hadn't heard of 'teenagers', but now they are a well-recognized section of society, with their own subculture, mores and even language. They are no longer 'overgrown children' or 'immature adults', but have carved out for themselves an accepted position in the social order. The same trend has set in for the elderly, but it is taking longer, because it is not easy to define 'old age', and people are not so keen to be labelled elderly as they are to be labelled young.

We shall return in a later chapter to consider the special contribution which the elderly can make to society, and the special relationship they can establish with the young, but here it is necessary to note a further fact that divides the age groups of society. I refer to the tremendous advances in technology during the last fifty years and more. It is very difficult for young people today to realize what the world was like before 1939. What my generation still regard as 'current affairs' are for the teenagers of today 'history' and barely 'modern history'. They can hardly imagine a world with which the over-seventies are familiar when there were no computers or television, and when radios (called 'wirelesses' in those days) and motor cars were a rarity. Writing on the subject of old age when he was seventy-two, Lord David Cecil said, 'I now realise that I belong to the past . . . I am no longer, as it were, a native of the age I live in.'

Nothing like the same amount of change took place in the eighty-five years before 1900 as has taken place since; and its scale and rapidity sometimes make the young and the old feel as if they inhabit different worlds. Even language presents difficulties, for words have changed their meaning. We are familiar with the way in which the word 'gay' has now been hijacked, and when used in its original and proper sense has to be qualified and explained. To 'make love' to the cook meant that you went into the kitchen to tell her how much you had enjoyed her meringues in the hope that she would make you some more. Now it means that you jump into bed with her. When I was young, a 'girlfriend' was someone you were courting, or 'walking out' with, but nowadays it is a euphemism for a 'mistress', someone with whom you are cohabiting, with or without the intention of eventually marrying. And it isn't only in the moral sphere that we meet this language barrier. 'Sensible' shoes, I discovered when teaching Scripture at Benenden, are what I have always rather prided myself on wearing, but what the modern teenage girl wouldn't like to be seen dead in. It is all very difficult!

Nor can the church—certainly not the Church of England anyway—claim to have helped to unify its members in this regard. Whatever we may think of *The Alternative Service Book* (and I happen to like a great deal of it) it has succeeded in splitting Anglican Christians into two groups. There are those, by no means exclusively the elderly, who prefer the old, traditional services, and those who want the new. It has thrown the clergy into disarray and confusion. Some will mix the services, having one on one Sunday and another on the next; while others, like our own in Crowborough where I live, will have two services each Sunday to suit all tastes. In the end, no doubt, the old people will die off and the new services will prevail; so while there is death there is hope so far as ultimate unity is concerned, but at a fairly grievous cost.

Yet this gap between the young and the very old can, as we will see, be very easily bridged. It is not the over-seventies against whom the teenagers are in revolt, but very often the middle-aged. With the really old they have a sort of natural affinity—'deep calling to deep'. But it needs a conscious effort on both sides. The young must break out of the mould which has been dictated for them by their particular peer group, and the elderly must take off the blinkers, and take Leonardo da Vinci's motto as their own: *'Nec lamentari, nec indignari, sed intelligere.'* (Neither weep, nor fume, but seek to understand.)

We must watch carefully for the tell-tale signs of senility, and find the sort of candid friend who will warn us when he sees them. It is all too easy for the elderly to become prolix, repetitive and verbose and to get into the habit of making a short story long. As a parson I am very frightened of this happening to me. A friend of mine speaking recently of a retired bishop and his sermons said, 'He is splendid for the first twenty minutes, but then . . .' I taught myself a salutary lesson the other day. I was recording a sermon on tape, when suddenly I fell asleep. I began to talk gibberish, then there was a pause, and then I woke up and continued. 'Golly,' I thought, 'if it has that effect on me . . .', and I was reminded of the sermon I once heard described as the perfect cure for insomnia.

It is very easy, too, for the elderly to become tediously reminiscent, and not to realize how quickly people can be bored with our stories and recollections, forgetting that while we may have all the time in the world, theirs is limited. Lord Randolph Churchill (Winston's father) was once sitting in his club when the club bore started off on some story. After a few minutes, Lord Randolph could stand it no longer, got up and rang the bell. When the waiter appeared he said, 'I have a train to catch, would you mind listening to the end of this story,' and walked out of the room. One can hardly blame him.

The other important thing to cultivate if we are to bridge the generation gap and win the confidence of the young is humility. Humility has been described as 'having the power you don't use'—the power to use our greater knowledge or experience to patronize, embarrass, humiliate and even snub other people. When some young person starts to tell a joke or a story we have often heard before, we shall not reveal the fact, or if we do it will be with great delicacy; and we won't try to cap it with one of our own.

One of the advantages the elderly have over the middle-aged is that they possess the time to listen to the very young and to take them seriously. They quickly sense this, and are surprised to discover how very 'modern' old people can be, and how sympathetic to the frustrations and problems which are worrying them. It is as though understanding sometimes skips a generation.

Paul Tournier, in the book referred to earlier, has a charming story about a very old Parisian lady who had been discussing the Sorbonne disturbances with her granddaughter in a very understanding and sympathetic way. 'How young you are, Grannie!' she exclaimed as she listened. It is this discovery which young people will make if they will give us a chance; while we in turn will catch something of the fire and enthusiasm of the teenagers. We dream dreams, and they see visions.

It is very easy to be critical of the young people of today, as almost every day we are reminded through the media of instances of vandalism, hooliganism, drug abuse and so on. Perhaps in different ways we were just as bad fifty years ago. It is difficult at this distance of time to remember. But while there may be much to deplore, there is one thing I have noticed over and over again about the young people of today, and that is that they *do care*. They care for animals, they care for little children, they care for each other, and, given a chance, they care for the elderly.

I say 'given a chance', because I think they are sometimes held back from expressing their concern by their own shyness and also by that fiercely proud independence which the aged are apt to exhibit—'I can manage, young man, I am not nearly as decrepit as you may suppose.'

I think this is a pity. For one thing we may live to regret it. In many ways very old people are like little children. We grow increasingly dependent upon the help that other people can provide, and if we insist upon retaining complete independence long after we are able to, we may well come to grief. And not to accept gratefully and humbly the help that the young, perhaps, are trying to offer is to deprive them of a form of service which they want to give; and if we do this, we strangle at birth the generous impulses we want to encourage.

I remember many years ago, long before there were such things as zebra crossings, I was standing on the kerbside of a busy road, waiting for the moment to cross. Suddenly I was aware of a very small boy standing beside me. 'Will you take me across the road?' he asked. So into my hand went his, and we threaded our way safely to the other side. One day I expect the roles to be reversed. It would be extremely foolish of me to launch out, waving a white stick, hoping for the best. I shall end up in hospital and on some motorist's conscience. When that day comes, I hope I shall not be too proud and independent to say to some young person standing near, 'Will you see me across the road?' For what a sad world this would be if there were no scope for the young to use their strength and compassion for the benefit of the old!

The loneliness of retirement and old age can of course be greatly eased by a really happy marriage —a genuine 'Darby and Joan' affair. But a word of warning: retirement can prove quite a strain upon a marriage. It may be exactly what both partners have been looking forward to, and even doing their best to hasten, but if it comes suddenly, or without sufficient forethought, it can have a disruptive effect. The wife, for example, who has established a pattern of life all of her own, and based upon her husband's working timetable, can be quite disoriented when she suddenly finds she has him around all day, dislocating the routine she has formed for herself and enjoyed for years.

The sensible couple will work this sort of problem out for themselves well in advance, and if they are wise will arrange a new daily and weekly programme by mutual agreement. It would be a mistake to abandon their own individual interests and their own particular circles of friends, and even the occasional separate holiday should not be regarded as an ominous prelude to disaster; indeed, I sometimes think marriages founder, not because husband and wife see too little of each other, but too much. Having said that, as a bachelor I have again and again been impressed with the serenity and richness that autumn brings to a marriage. I always like Agatha Christie's remark, that she found it so nice being married to an archaeologist, because the older she grew, the more interested he became in her.

For the bachelor, as he grows old, there is the

opposite danger. He can become too content with his own company, his home a moated castle; a bit of a recluse, perhaps, the prisoner of a routine, a domestic pedant, a perfectionist, for whom there is a place for everything, and everything must be in its right place. He is slightly resentful, though he tries not to show it, of unscheduled interruptions, and easily thrown by the arrival, the noise and the untidiness of children. But it is to be hoped that long before he retires he has dealt firmly with these tendencies; for we need to remember that what we are at fifty we will still be, only very much more so, at seventy.

There is, of course, one particularly distressing form of loneliness which must almost inevitably accompany old age, and that is when one partner of a very happy marriage dies. Usually it is the woman who is left alone, and the sudden break after forty or fifty years of domestic bliss is stunning in its effect. No wonder people say, 'I just can't accept it. I feel he is still around. I expect him to walk through the door at any moment.'

However much a woman may take it for granted that she will outlive a husband several years her senior in age, the sense of loss when it actually comes is overwhelming. It can be aggravated too by the fact that she may have to leave the home where they were living together, and even find herself financially embarrassed; while some of the people she knew because they were friends of her husband may not be quite so inclined to continue their friendship with her. True, she may still be young enough to take up a career, perhaps abandoned since her marriage, and even to marry again; but these are not thoughts that will occur to her, if they occur at all, until many months later. Meanwhile she is 'retired' in a double sense from the happiness of her marriage and from the work and interests she was able to share with her husband.

The only complete answer to loneliness is a spiritual one. 'Religion,' said someone, 'is what a man does with his loneliness.' If that means that religion is simply a solitary relationship with God, and has no outward, evangelistic or social dimension, then it is demonstrably false; but if it means that the one great consoling influence in times of loneliness and distress is the sustaining presence of God, then it is a profoundly true statement.

It was my privilege recently to see a letter from someone who has been in an African prison, in the most miserable conditions, for ten years, and not for anything she has done wrong. It was most moving to hear what she had to say about the goodness of God and her faith in him. I couldn't help wondering what my reaction would be in similar circumstances, and with apparently so little hope of eventual release.

I was reminded of Madame Guyon, a saintly French noblewoman who was falsely accused and wrongly imprisoned for ten years in 1688. While in prison she wrote these words, which Joni Eareckson quotes in her book *A Step Further*.

> A little bird I am
> Shut from the fields of air;
> And in my cage I sit and sing
> To him who placed me there;
> Well pleased a prisoner to be,
> Because, my God, it pleases thee.
>
> Naught have I else to do;
> I sing the whole day long;

> And he whom most I love to please,
> Doth listen to my song;
> He caught and bound my wandering wing,
> But still he bends to hear me sing.
>
> My cage confines me round;
> Abroad I cannot fly,
> But though my wing is closely bound
> My heart's at liberty;
> My prison walls cannot control
> The flight, the freedom of the soul.
>
> Oh! it is good to soar
> These bolts and bars above,
> To him whose purpose I adore,
> Whose providence is love;
> And in thy mighty will to find
> The joy, the freedom, of the mind.

There are many different kinds of prisoner, and these words have a message for those whose freedom and activity is restricted by the weakness and infirmity of old age just as much as those who languish behind stone walls and iron bars.

Financial

We have already considered that curious paradox which allows quite wealthy people to imagine that they are verging on bankruptcy, and even to live in a state of unnecessarily degrading poverty; but there are many people for whom the problem—real, and not imaginary—is exactly the opposite. How can they stretch their slender means to cover their daily needs?

Successive governments have done something to help. The lifting of the earnings limit is a relief, for it enables the able-bodied to supplement their income without reducing their pension; and the index-linking of the pensions themselves at least ensures that they keep pace with the cost of living.

But old people are very vulnerable when it comes to money matters, often through sheer ignorance. Thousands, for example, fail to exercise their right to claim supplementary benefit; while others often pay more tax than they should, because it seems to be a rule of the game that the Inland Revenue will point out mistakes if it is of benefit to them to do so, but regard it as the taxpayer's responsibility to discover those that might favour him. It really does pay to take advice, and this need not be expensive, because nearly always living somewhere near is a retired banker or Inland Revenue official who will be happy to help. My next-door neighbour used to be a retired income-tax inspector, and he was a great help to people, a gamekeeper turned poacher.

Then again, old people are very easily exploited, and there are, I am afraid, plenty of unscrupulous people about who are ready to take advantage of them. Some old lady in her eighties, for example, is persuaded to part with some of her silverware at a ridiculously low price by the charm and chatter of some specious door-to-door salesman; or to put some of her hard-earned savings into a completely spurious investment or insurance policy. Let me hasten to add that I have always been greatly impressed with the way in which representatives of reputable life assurance companies and the Stock Exchange work. They would rather (and sometimes do) suffer loss themselves than take advantage of the ignorant or the gullible.

The fact that so many people now own the

houses they occupy, and that the value of these houses is increasing all the time, means that far more people than ever before must be called 'capitalists' (in that they have capital assets), and this in turn means that they should make a will. Many people hesitate to do so, in the superstitious belief, perhaps, that it will bring death nearer. But that, of course, is nonsense, while not to make a will, and to die intestate, can put everyone to extra trouble, and even lead to family quarrels which can drag on for years—as in *Bleak House*— and create very bad blood between relations who up to that point have been quite friendly.

There are, I know, those who disagree with the whole idea of inherited wealth, but while respecting this viewpoint, it is one I have never been able to share. Passages in the Bible like 2 Corinthians 12:14 and Proverbs 9:14 do seem to me to justify the transmission of wealth from one generation to the next. No one will argue against the idea that extreme inequality of wealth is intolerable, or fail to accept with a good grace those taxes which are designed to distribute it more evenly; but I can see no good reason why children and other, perhaps needy, close relatives should not benefit from what is ultimately disposable; and I have always felt that the bulk of any capital I may leave should go to the family rather than to charitable organizations, chiefly because it was probably family money in the first place. In this regard I think it is fair to say that charity begins at home.

We talk about 'possessing money', but one of the things we have to be careful about, not least in old age, is that we do not allow it to possess us. Money is like a very powerful drug. Used in the right way, it can do untold good; but the Bible warns us in many places (e.g. 1 Tim 6:9-10) of the trouble and sorrow it can bring into our lives if we allow the accumulation of it to become one of our principal aims. The ancient Egyptians were often buried with their treasures beside them, in case they were needed in the next life. But we know that is impossible. 'We brought nothing into this world, and it is certain that we can carry nothing out' (1 Tim 6:7). The following conversation is supposed to have taken place between two elderly members in a London club; 'I see old Charles's will is in the paper today.'

'Is that so? What did he leave?'

'Everything.'

Of course, this is not to say that as we grow old we should become careless about money, or regard it as of no importance, for the Christian should always find that used wisely and prayerfully it will increase his capacity to do good. Most elderly people begin to find that their personal needs decrease with the years (which is one reason why it is so difficult to find anything useful to give them at Christmas) and that they have more to give away to those in need and to charitable organizations; and I believe that it is very often in old age that we begin to experience the truth of Jesus' words when he said, 'Happiness lies more in giving than in receiving' (Acts 20:35, New English Bible).

The Temptations of Old Age

When I was a child
The devil's great plan
Was to make me pretend
That I was a man.
But now I am old,
I'll not be beguiled
By his efforts to make me
Behave like a child.

Robert Buchanan

Next to the very young, I suppose the very old are the most selfish.

Thackeray

Theodore Roosevelt, said one of his children, always liked to be the centre of any situation. 'When he went to a wedding, he wanted to be the bride. When he went to a funeral, he was sorry if he could not be the corpse.'

He who falls in love with himself at least has this consolation: that he need fear no rivals.

Franklin

I complained because I had no shoes until I met a man who had no feet.

Arab proverb

Doubt is not the opposite of faith, but an element of it.
Paul Tillich

Doubt your doubts before you doubt your beliefs.
Walt Allmand

For it came to pass, when Solomon was old, that his wives turned away his heart after other gods: and his heart was not perfect with the Lord his God, as was the heart of David his father.
1 Kings 11:4

5

The Temptations of Old Age

There must be many different and equally valid ways of interpreting and applying the account of Jesus' temptations, but I always remember one that was pointed out to me many years ago. If we follow the order in which the temptations occur in St Luke's gospel (which is different from Matthew's), the suggestion is that they may apply to different periods of life.

The first temptation concerns the turning of stones into bread, a direct appeal to our appetites, and the thought is that this applies to the temptations of youth; for it is then that the young Christian has chiefly to do battle with the sins of the flesh, the physical appetites of greed, lust and desire, and needs with God's help to learn the all-important lesson of self-control and self-discipline.

This is not to suggest that the sins of the flesh are any worse or even as bad as the sins of the disposition. It is worth remembering that in the story of the prodigal son, it was not he, but his elder brother who ended up outside the father's house; and Jesus was always more severe on those who exhibited pride and self-righteousness than upon those who gave way to lust. The harlots and publicans of his day were further up the queue than the pharisees when it came to entering the kingdom of heaven. Nor must we suppose that adulthood or even old age immunizes us from those earlier temptations. Far from it. It was in middle age that David committed adultery with Bathsheba.

Perhaps the importance of these early battles is that if they can be won, it makes further conquests of our great enemy more probable in the future; for we must remember that while temptations may change their form, their force will not diminish. Satan may vary his tactics, but never his overall strategic aim which is to knock us out of the fight altogether. The temptations which assail us at sixteen will be different from but no fiercer than those we have to face at sixty. At sixteen the prevailing wind may be from the east and at sixty from the west; but that is the only difference.

The second temptation which Jesus had to face was Satan's attempt to persuade him to compromise, to sacrifice principles for ambitions—'Seek first the kingdom of Satan, and all these things will be added to you.' Ambition rather than appetite is now the target: 'Adopt this practice, change this stance, modify this attitude if you really want to get on and reach the top.' I have met men who, when faced with this sort of temptation, have felt that the only course open to them was to pull out altogether and resign quite a lucrative position: 'I was told that I could only expect to get on and gain promotion if I was prepared to fall in with a line of conduct which I felt to be wrong.' What courage it needs to stand out in that way!

The third temptation, it is suggested, is one which applies especially to the elderly and retired. You remember that Jesus was asked to cast himself down from the temple roof, and in this way justify his claims to be the Messiah, and win the applause and approbation of the people for himself and his cause. Very often, I think, this sort of temptation comes to people in old age, not to do anything dramatic, of course, but to seek to justify themselves and what they have done; to win the recognition and approval which they feel may have been denied them in earlier life. Memoirs and autobiographies appear intended to 'put the record straight', and to prove that what seemed at the time to be a dismal disaster was in fact a minor triumph, and would have been recognized as such, but for someone else's blunders. Of course, we all love recognition, however belated it may be; but there is something slightly pathetic about the old man who seems desperately anxious to justify himself, and to tell us why he never became a Cabinet minister, or why he never received (or perhaps declined to accept) the offer of a knighthood. Moreover, in old age he is running out of contemporaries who can challenge his assertions; but he is surely forgetting the injunction of Scripture, 'Let another man praise thee, and not thine own mouth' (Prov 27:2).

Very often this sort of craving for approbation is accompanied by regret, because we know failure to have been largely our own fault. The might-have-been perhaps would have been if we had played our cards differently and more wisely; and we have to learn to live with what we were and not what we would like to have been. Perhaps this is why Seneca said, 'Call no man happy until he is dead.'

Everyone is familiar with Disraeli's famous remark, 'Youth is a blunder; Manhood a struggle; Old Age a regret.' There is certainly this amount of truth in it, namely that few of us reach old age without regrets, and the wish that we could re-live parts of our lives again, scaling heights, avoiding pitfalls, winning battles we lacked the skill or courage or even inclination to attempt in real life. This is the stuff of which nightmares are made, and calls for that memory-management of which we thought in an earlier chapter. The tragedy is when we allow these regrets to spill over into our attitudes and relationships, and spoil life for ourselves and other people. It can do so in several ways.

Egotism

If self-indulgence is the weakness of youth, and self-interest that of manhood, then surely self-importance is the failing of old age. I am not thinking here of the pomposity we sometimes find in newly-appointed Cabinet ministers, bishops, or headmasters, who have not quite got used to their exalted position, nor made up their minds which pose to adopt. I am thinking rather of the self-importance of the child who sees himself at the centre of his little world, and thinks that it exists for his benefit.

Old age and childhood do not simply enjoy affinity, there is a similarity between them, as the phrase 'second childhood' suggests. The child's world has not yet expanded, while that of the elderly has begun to shrink. The child has not yet left his harbour, and the old man is approaching his.

It is for this reason that old people can become very selfish, expecting everyone to conform to their wishes, their needs and their plans; and when they don't get what they want, or are kept waiting for it, they can become sour and cantankerous. Of course it is the duty of the next generation to humour them as much as possible, but now and then a metaphorical smack may be the best thing for them. There is a splendid old man whom I know, now approaching the age of a hundred, and loved by those who know him. His inevitably shrinking world includes the Somme, where he was wounded, but he has to be restrained from physically attacking those who leave litter in the Memorial Garden.

I sometimes tell children that there are two great families in the world, and everyone belongs to one or the other. The name of one is 'Me-First' and the name of the other is 'After-You'. If we can make sure fairly early in life that we are firmly adopted by the second, then we shall have gone a long way towards avoiding the sort of self-centredness and self-importance which can spoil old age, and add greatly to its difficulties.

Pessimism

There are probably no two phrases which you will hear more often on the lips of the elderly than these: 'Things are not what they were,' and 'I don't know what the world is coming to.' I am afraid I don't argue, as perhaps I should, but smile weakly and acquiesce.

Of course in one sense every Christian is a pessimist, because we can see no hope for the world apart from Christ. The facile optimism of Edwardian days has gone for ever. Few would agree with what Arthur Balfour said in 1908, that 'There are, so far, no symptoms of pause or regression in the onward movement which for more than a thousand years has been characteristic of our civilization.' It was a kinsman of Lord Balfour's, Lord David Cecil, who went nearer the mark some thirty years later when he said, 'Barbarism is not behind us, it is beneath us'— ready, that is, to break out at any moment.

But when I am asked whether I think the world is getting better or worse, I am bound to say 'both'. In many respects it has to be admitted that 'things are not what they were'. Crime, we are told, is on the increase, and so are vandalism and terrorism. Drug abuse was practically unheard of before the war, and the divorce rate a fraction of what it is now. The 'fear of the Lord' which imposed moral restraints a hundred or even fifty years ago no longer holds the sway it did, and standards have therefore dropped accordingly.

On the other hand, think of the improvements, and not just in material terms. Slavery has been abolished, and there has been a dramatic advance in the care of the sick, the aged, the handicapped and deprived. Children are no longer exploited as once they were, the pillory disappeared when Queen Victoria came to the throne, and it is now over a hundred years since we last had a public execution.

This paradox is precisely what Jesus himself led us to expect. Asked in the form of a parable whether it was his intention to root out the evil from the world, he replied, 'No! . . . Let the wheat and the weeds both grow together until harvest' (Mt 13:24-30 GNB). And that is what we see happening. The good and the evil are coexisting, and more than that, they are growing or increasing together. The pessimist looks only at the black squares on the chessboard, and the optimist at the white squares; but the Christian, who is a realist, looks at both at the same time, and sees that in the wisdom of God both are inseparable until the end of what we call time. 'The optimist proclaims that we live in the best of all possible worlds; and the pessimist fears this is true,' said J.B. Cabell. The Christian, on the other hand, realizes that things are not as bad as they might be if God were to lose control; but not as good as they will be when he asserts complete control.

From time to time we meet people with this gloomy, pessimistic outlook on life, who seem to have lost hope. To be in their presence for any length of time is a depressing experience, like standing around in a drizzle without an umbrella. Such people need to be reminded of the many things God has given them to enjoy, of the triumphs he is gaining in different parts of the world. It is true that 'now we see not yet all things put under him. But we see Jesus . . .' who has already won the victory (Heb 2:8-9). In July 1940, the Germans had a saying, 'The war is won, but it is not yet over'. How wrong they were, we now know; but the words exactly describe the position in which the Christian church finds itself today.

Sentimentalism

I always remember an occasion at school when a somewhat histrionic master swept into the room and announced that he had been trying to find the true meaning of the word 'sentimental'. There was of course the form 'wag' who asked him very solemnly if he had looked it up in the dictionary—a suggestion which brought an exclamation and gesture of disgust. A discussion then followed and it was agreed that a sentimentalist was someone who attached a value to something which was intrinsically false.

Every material thing has at least three values: the commercial value—that is, what it will fetch in the marketplace; the intrinsic value—what, if that is discoverable, it is really worth; and the sentimental value—what it is worth to me because of the subjective attachment I feel for the article concerned. Now it is this sort of value which grows with the years, and is apt, unless we are aware of it and take it into account, to distort our judgement. Things which are of little real value mean a great deal to the elderly, because of personal and family associations. It is this which makes the theft of some trophy like a medal or a cup, of no great value in itself, so hurtful, because it meant so much to the owner.

Now of course there is nothing wrong with this if we keep things in perspective, but where it can become dangerous in old people is in their tendency to sentimentalize the past, and it is partly this that leads to the pessimism we have just been considering. It is easy to read *Kilvert's Diary,* for example, and to wallow in his inimitable descriptions of slow, gentle, sweet-scented country life. It is less easy to remember that for many people they were harsh, primitive times, and that he himself died at an early age of appendicitis, because at that time they did not know how to perform an operation which today would have kept him in hospital for less than a week.

All elderly people tend to look at the past through rose-tinted spectacles. It is one of the quirks of memory to erase our least pleasant recollections. Our childhood was probably never quite as happy as we have persuaded ourselves and now like to believe it was. I am writing these words during the wettest August we have had for years, genuinely convinced that it hardly ever rained in August before the war.

It is therefore important that the elderly should not lose touch with reality by living nostalgically in an idealized past of their own creation; for if they lose touch with the reality of their own past, they are likely to fall out of step with the rising generations, and consequently not be taken seriously or trusted when they talk about other things, and so widen the gap which they want to bridge.

Scepticism

I am not now thinking of that sad experience which we considered earlier, when Christians seem to lose their faith, and having been such an inspiration and help to others in earlier years, spend their own closing days in darkness and doubt. I am thinking of that attitude towards other people and life in general which has grown disillusioned, which loses faith in human nature, and slips back into apathy and indifference. It is the attitude of mind we find permeating the book of Ecclesiastes. Everything that people value and pursue is a mere 'chasing of the wind', and the preacher concludes, 'Vanity of vanities . . . all is vanity'.

Faced with the apparent triumph of evil in the world, we shrug our shoulders and ask what we can do about it anyway. What is the point of giving money to the starving millions in Africa when we hear that so much is diverted to other ends by corrupt governments? What difference will our prayers make? How can our tiny contribution to the sum total of good hold back the long, drawling tides of hatred and evil sweeping across the world?

Statesmen and politicians all over the world seem powerless in the face of war and terrorism, famine and unemployment. Summit meetings and conferences are called, but it is not surprising that old people lose faith in them. They have seen it all before, and it has led nowhere —simply 'a chasing of the wind'. And with that same despondent philosopher they would say, 'What has happened before will happen again. What has been done before will be done again. There is nothing new in the whole world. "Look," they say, "here is something new!" But no, it has all happened before, long before we were born' (Eccles 1:9 GNB).

But old people must not abandon their faith in God's power to influence world affairs. The world needs their prayers and their efforts, such as they are; and if they opt out, they are imperilling the future of their children and grandchildren.

Cynicism

Scepticism will very quickly lead to cynicism, a less desirable state of mind still; for the cynic not only questions the ability of people to act, but their motives as well. If for instance I advised you not to write your memoirs because I doubted your ability to do so effectively, that would be sceptical; but if I implied that you should not do so because you wanted people to believe better than the truth about you, then that would by cynical. Pessimism is the absence of hope, scepticism is an absence of faith, by cynicism is worst of all, because it is the absence of love.

In the minds of elderly people it sometimes works in this way. They are disappointed because their advice is not sought as they would like, or because it is suggested to them that they should resign from a certain committee, and the temptation comes to impute to those responsible unworthy motives. 'They've gone all trendy'; 'They are no longer as sound as they were'; 'They don't like my views'; 'Look at the sort of people they turn to now.' But all the time the truth is simpler and much less sinister. Their advice is no longer asked, because it is utterly predictable, it can be taken for granted and therefore need no longer be sought; while by holding on to their place on the committee they are blocking the way for some promising younger person to join it. Admittedly these facts are sometimes conveyed in a tactless and heartless manner by those who forget how sensitive, and even touchy, elderly people can be, and how readily they take offence.

Of course a little gentle, humorous cynicism is

one thing, but like sarcasm, if it is allowed to colour our whole attitude to life and our personal relationships, it can have a most corrosive effect on ourselves as well as on others; and if the elderly allow their disappointments and frustrations to drive them along this road, they will find it is the quickest and shortest way there is to lose the friends they have.

These then are some of the temptations which are perhaps peculiar to the elderly. We must not suppose, as we have noted already, that those temptations which attacked us in our youth or adulthood will leave us completely alone, but with the passage of time the appetites of the flesh begin to diminish; while envy, jealousy and covetousness—the principal enemies of competitive manhood—seem to lose something of their earlier power. It is in our attitudes towards people, events and circumstances that we can grow sweet or sour.

What is the secret of success? Surely it must lie in the closest possible walk with our Lord Jesus Christ. It is worth reading his life again specially to note the absence of those destructive and caustic influences we have been considering. Was there ever anyone less egotistical, or who more completely lived up to the motto, 'After You'? He was the perfect realist in whom not a trace of sentimentality could be found. He never lost hope or faith in God or in the recoverability of man. And 'having loved his own which were in the world, he loved them unto the end' (Jn 13:1).

I often think what a privilege it would have been to have had Socrates or Solomon, Drake or Nelson as a close and intimate friend. Their wisdom or courage must have been contagious, and you could not have lived with them for long and remained stupid or cowardly. Surely that is how it should be with us and Jesus Christ. If he is our companion, and communicates with us through prayer and Bible reading, meditation and worship, will not something of the beauty of his character rub off on to us? It is this that gives old age, as I have seen many times, its true loveliness.

The Contributions of Old Age—1

Do you remember, Lord, how I,
A proud and wayward youth,
Came in the morning of my life
To know and love your truth?

Then as the years sped past and I
Became a man so soon,
How graciously you guided me
Through the long afternoon?

Now as the shadows start to fall,
Grant that there may be still
Some evening work for me to do,
Some purpose to fulfil.

Buchanan

Those who love deeply never grow old; they may die of
old age, but they die young.

Ladies' Home Journal

Old age hath yet his honour and his toil,
Death closes all; but something ere the end,

Some work of noble note may yet be done.

Tennyson

All who deserve his love he makes his own;
And to be loved himself, needs only to be known.

Dryden

Therefore my age is as a lusty winter
Frosty, but kind.

Shakespeare

Old men should be explorers.

Roethke

May I grow lovely growing old,
So many fine things do;
Silver and ivory and gold
And silks need not be new;
And there is healing in old trees,
Old streets a glamour hold,
Why may not I, as well as these,
Grow lovely, growing old?

I, who am an elder myself, appeal to the church elders among you . . . to be shepherds of the flock that God gave you and to take care of it willingly, as God wants you to, and not unwillingly.

1 Pet 5:1-2, GNB

6

The Contributions of Old Age—1

We saw in an earlier chapter the importance of cultivating interests, hobbies and forms of activity well in advance of retirement, and to see them, not just as a way of passing the time and keeping boredom at bay, but also as a means of developing the personality and widening the mind. Education, in the broadest sense, continues until death, for there is infinitely more knowledge available than the human mind can appreciate or absorb in the course of a lifetime. 'The dreaming eyes of wonder' which we noted in the child should still be as sharp when we reach the age of seventy or eighty, and as capable of being awestruck.

But unless we intend to take up these pursuits to an almost professional level, they will remain as hobbies and interests, and we must not be surprised if they fail to satisfy us as anything more. What was considered to be the perfect way of spending a holiday, or a weekly half-day, may very well pall if we find it to be the only activity we are qualified to enjoy. We all know that experience which comes when some mild complaint keeps us in bed for a few days, or we are convalescing from an operation. We arm ourselves with all the books we have been waiting for an opportunity to read. But invariably we find that given so much time to read, the inclination to do so is strictly limited, and we begin to pine for some other way of passing the day.

Therefore, the person who retires in good health, and with ample reserves of energy and vigour, will want something more than unlimited gardening or golf. He will want to do something which makes use of the gifts he has exercised for so long in his job, and with which he can continue to make a useful contribution to society. I am not thinking of the 'second career' which many middle-aged people have to seek, perhaps when they leave the armed services at forty-five or fifty, or are made redundant. For them it is necessary to continue to earn a living. I am thinking of the man or woman who can afford to work voluntarily, asking for nothing beyond his expenses, and is anxious to undertake some really useful work, but free from the pressures which were involved when he had to earn his living. Of course, he may still find it necessary to earn, but in that case I do not regard him as truly retired, for the essence of retirement is that at last you become your own master and can set the parameters within which you want to work.

It is often at this stage of life that a man or a woman will be at their most useful—'re-tyred', as someone put it to me, and with plenty of mileage ahead. There is an almost unlimited number of charitable organizations, church societies, local clubs and institutions which would collapse or be seriously damaged if it were not for the continual stream of voluntary helpers from the ranks of the retired. We have already thought of the retired income-tax inspector who was willing to assist people with their annual returns. The person who has learnt some skill or craft can also make a very valuable contribution to society by trying to impart it to others. Others who have travelled, or are expert ornithologists or astronomers—there are a host of other subjects—could well train themselves as lecturers at schools or other institutions on their particular subject.

Doctors, clergymen and schoolteachers are particularly fortunate in this respect. They can plan an ordered retreat from their full-time occupation. My father, like me, was a clergyman, and for various reasons he retired at the age of fifty—the age, incidentally, at which the Old Testament priesthood, the Levites, were obliged to 'retire from regular service and . . . serve no longer' (Num 8:25, New English Bible). But I think some of his most useful work was done during the remaining twenty-five years of his life. He was in constant demand as a preacher, and supervised the building of a new church in Camberley. Another great friend of mine continued his voluntary, unofficial ministry until he was nearly eighty, and was indignant when anyone asked him about his retirement. 'Clergy never retire', he would snap. Nor did he, until overtaken in the last year or two of his life by failing health. My own doctor, saddened at having to give up his work as a GP, has made himself indispensable at a healing and convalescent centre in this part of the world.

What I will call 'occupied retirement' gives us the opportunity for a second innings, even if it is on a limited over basis. For this reason it is wise not to defer retirement too long, or we may run out of energy and enthusiasm, or find that there are no 'overs' left.

Here again, as in the case of hobbies and other interests, it is necessary to prepare ourselves before we retire, not perhaps in any training we undertake, because I am assuming that our contribution will be conditioned by our previous career, but in our attitude of mind. The self-centred person who has never reached out to help others is not suddenly going to develop a great sense of altruism at the age of sixty-five. The direction our lives take at that age will be determined by the course we have set for ourselves many years before; and at the age of retirement it may be too late for the leopard to change his spots (Jer 13:23).

Of course the Christian is at a tremendous advantage when it comes to this 'second innings', simply because there is an extra dimension in which he can offer to work. Perhaps his job has been somewhat routine, even frustrating, however necessary for the security and welfare of his family. Now suddenly he is at liberty to follow his most heartfelt inclinations. He looks round his home-church and begins to see what a lively contribution he can make. His gifts as an administrator, a financier, a speaker, or a personnel manager or salesman are all available and can be sublimated into Christian service.

Quite recently I was talking with a clergyman, a nephew of mine, about unemployment. We were discussing why it was that it never became a real issue and seemed to make so little impact on voters at the general election in 1983. Is it today the harrowing and desperately frustrating experience it is often made out to be, and certainly was in the 1930s? Clearly among young people this must be so; for to leave school in some parts of the country with a one-in-four chance of finding a job is a prospect which no decent society can tolerate as an acceptable state of affairs for long.

He then went on to tell me of a man in his previous parish in Sheffield who had been genuinely pleased to be made redundant. His work consisted of one of those soul-destroying jobs where a man simply does something for which the necessary piece of machinery has not yet been invented. He was fortunate in that his wife had a steady job, and he himself saw the opportunity at last of undertaking voluntary work in connection with his church and neighbourhood for which in the past he had had neither the time nor the energy.

This is obviously a very exceptional case, but it does illustrate my point that a person's job can actually stand in the way of what he really wants to do, and that retirement (sometimes taken early), and in certain circumstances redundancy, can open more doors than it closes.

What is really sad is when such people are allowed to continue to feel unfulfilled and, worse still, unwanted. They are too valuable to be left on the shelf, and it is up to the church to organize itself in such a way as to make the fullest possible use of the talents offered to it by its retired members. It is tragic when, as sometimes happens, we meet a person who says, 'I offered my services to such-and-such a society or organization. I was trained to do just the sort of job they seemed to want done, and was willing to do it for nothing. They smiled nicely, wrote politely, but I have heard no more.' Can the church really afford to do without such people? I know it must bring on and develop the young, and prepare them for responsibility, but surely there is so much to be done that every willing volunteer should be mobilized.

I remember hearing of a university professor during the war for whose undoubted gifts the powers-that-be seemed unable to discover a useful outlet; he ended up in charge of a mobile bath-unit in Madagascar. What a pathetic waste! But sometimes, I am afraid, the church shows as little imagination as that in the use it makes of its available manpower.

It is not only in offering their particular skills and attributes, those in which they have been trained, that elderly Christians can make such a valuable contribution to society and the church; for old age brings with it that most valuable of all commodities—time. For once 'time is on our side'. We are no longer 'summoned by bells'. We can make our own programme and timetable, and even after the sort of voluntary work we have been considering, and the leisure activities we enjoy, there is time for us to use profitably for the benefit of other people. Much will of course depend upon our particular aptitudes and circumstances, but let us consider some of the forms of Christian service which we may be able to pursue.

Speaking

I am thinking here of the specifically Christian

opportunities which come to those of us who have retired, lay-people as well as clergy. We have more time at our disposal and are in a better position to accept invitations. I found that in the first year after my retirement I actually did more speaking than in the last year before I retired, and I expect this is the experience of many clergymen and others.

However, I do think there is a tendency amongst some younger Christian leaders to write off those of us who are growing old as out of touch with the young people of today—good, perhaps, when it comes to addressing elderly congregations, but unsuitable for more youthful assemblies. It has to be said at once that sometimes, perhaps quite often, they are right, for there are certain traps into which elderly preachers can all too easily fall, and we shall look at these presently; but I do not think they are right as often as they suppose.

I was fascinated to watch the first debate that was ever televised from the House of Lords. It was generally agreed that Harold Macmillan, by then well into his eighties, completely stole the show. It was interesting to try to analyse the secret of his mastery. There was of course sheer technical brilliance, born of long years of experience. He is, as all orators have to be, a consummate actor. When Garrick was asked by Bishop Butler why he himself was so much less successful in holding the attention of an audience than Garrick, the actor is said to have replied, 'Because, my Lord, you preach fact as if it were fiction, and I preach fiction as if it were fact.' But I believe it was something more than Macmillan's gift as a spellbinder that kept me glued to my chair that afternoon. It was the almost tangible respect and authority which attached to his great age. There was the feeling that he was above and beyond the petty party squabbles of the day, that he could safely indulge in a certain mischievous playfulness which delighted his audience, and opened their minds to the more serious things he had to say. He had nothing to lose, and he could expose his innermost thoughts with a frankness which would not have been possible twenty years before.

I had another interesting example of the same thing only the other day. I was talking to the chaplain of a well-known independent secondary school. It is their custom at this particular school to have a series of talks, a kind of 'mini-mission' during the Lent Term. In recent years the chaplain had invited several very gifted young men to speak —'whizz-kids', as he described them, though not unkindly; but then, for a change, he invited a clergyman in his late seventies. He described to me how this 'little old man, in a rather scruffy pullover and a slightly frayed suit' had gripped the school night after night in a way which the younger men were quite unable to do.

We discussed the matter at some length, trying to discover the reason. It may have been partly that some of the younger men tried to be too intellectual, feeling, perhaps, that they had to make an impression; while the older man, on the other hand, was less inhibited in speaking straight from the heart, and drawing upon a much longer Christian experience. In a sense he had more in common with his hearers than the younger men, because he had more to share with them. It is possible that if you were to read afterwards what was said at the time, you would be far more impressed with the talks given by the younger men. But sermons are not spoken essays, and so much turns on the direct, personal contact. In a curious way you feel more affinity with someone sitting on the opposite bank of the river to yourself than you do with someone who is still struggling to cross the bridge. I remember a Labour Member of Parliament once telling me that he found he got on more easily with members of the opposition than he did with those of his own party, 'Because I am not in competition with them.' There is a sense in which that is true of retired people. Their reputation is no longer at stake, and they could not care less what other people think of them. It would be quite unfair to suggest that younger speakers are always thinking of the effect they are creating, and that older people never do so. All I am saying is that as we grow old the reason for doing so gets less, and perhaps the temptation does too.

From my own experience, I think it is true to say that I seem to be able to hold the attention of young people today better than I could twenty years ago; but that may be that the sixties were a notoriously difficult time for preachers, when teen-agers just did not want to listen. At the same time I think it has something to do with the respect which is still, I believe, innately felt by the young for 'the hoary head'.

But, as I have already said, and quite apart from the fact that not everyone is equipped for public speaking, there are traps into which the elderly are very apt to fall. I refer to them as the 'Three R's'—Rambling, Reminiscence and Repetition.

Almost the first three things a speaker has to

learn are to 'Stand up, Speak up and Shut up'; and it is interesting that the elderly are apt to fall at these hurdles in the reverse order: once they get going, they are often very hard to stop.

My old headmaster was renowned for the length of his sermons, and I think his record was generally held to be thirty-three minutes. During the war, after his retirement and when he was over seventy, he was asked back to teach at the school of which he had been headmaster before he came to us—Haileybury. He chose a very hot June morning for an attempt on his own record, but the congregation were having none of it, and developed a communal cough which finally reduced him to premature silence. But he was to have the last laugh. No sooner was the service over, than there was a head-long rush for the swimming-pool, but the head-master had got there first, and there was a notice on the door to say that 'Owing to the cough which is afflicting the school today, the swimming-pool is closed'.

I have reverted in old age to the practice which I had never entirely abandoned, but observed very closely as a curate, that of writing out my sermons in full. It does not always mean (though perhaps more often than not it does) that I take the manu-script into the pulpit with me, but I find that the discipline does prevent my becoming verbose, and I can know in advance exactly how long the sermon will last. If allowance is made for minor deviations, I don't think it need be restrictive; and after all, if a thing is worth saying at all, it is surely worth saying in the best possible way. This may come naturally and spontaneously to younger minds, but when we grow old *le mot juste* is apt to forsake us at the critical moment, and as a result we fumble and ramble and become unnecessarily prolix. 'Has the preacher finished?' asked a latecomer to church one day. 'Ay,' replied the verger, 'he's finished all right, but he can't stop.'

One of the favourite radio programmes during the war was 'The Brains' Trust'. Four or five experts dealt amusingly and eruditely with listeners' questions. I remember having one of mine answered on one occasion. The team nearly always included a certain Commander Campbell who had obviously sailed the seven seas in his earlier days and knew every corner of the world. His favourite opening gambit seemed to be, 'When I was in Patagonia,' and it became a kind of radio joke, though I don't think many people knew where Patagonia was. But the phrase became useful shorthand, and I remember on one occasion I had to brief a bishop about a sermon he was to preach to a great crowd of schoolmasters. Knowing his penchant for story telling, I wrote and suggested that there should not be too much 'when I was in Patagonia'. He laughed, took the point, and we had an excellent sermon.

It is natural for old people to reminisce. After all, they have a much longer past than future, and so much of their experience can usefully and profitably be shared with others. But it is something that needs watching. It can be boring ('Here we go again!'), it can be egotistical ('Always talking about himself!') and it can lead to the rambling verbosity we have already considered.

The third danger is repetition. In the company of my older friends I often find myself listening to the same story over and over again, and I have no doubt that I am as guilty as they. This is a very tiresome habit for the preacher to get into. I don't mean that he will repeat himself in the same talk. That really is a sign of senility, but it can be guarded against by the kind of careful preparation I have suggested. But speaking next Sunday he may forget what he said to the same people three weeks ago. This applies particularly to stories, anecdotes and illustrations which are very often remembered when what they were intended to teach is forgotten. Again, we can protect ourselves by careful preparation; and sometimes when I am in doubt as to whether or not I am repeating myself, I deliberately say, 'You will probably have heard this story from me before, but I would like to refer to it again.' That defuses what might otherwise be a gaffe.

There is also the danger of the elderly Christian preacher's becoming obsessed with one or two pet subjects. I suppose it is all part of the hardening and narrowing process which effects muscles and arteries. We concentrate more and more on less and less. And there are preachers who, however carefully you brief them, will end up on their particular hobbyhorse. I believe it is one of the chief reasons why elderly people are sometimes disappointed when they are not invited to speak somewhere. 'Yes, he is a good speaker, but he can't keep off the subject of drink, or sex, or money, or whatever it is.' It is a very tiresome form of repetition.

Allowing for these three dangers, though, the elderly have an enormous amount to give, because they can speak from such a wealth of experience as well as, it is to be hoped, from many more years of study and reading. They are like the 'householder' in the story (Mt 13:52). 'which bringeth forth out of his treasure things new and old'. There is a shop near here called 'Bygones' which sells all kinds of things which belong to an age that is past; and probably all of us have had the experience of calling on the very elderly and enjoying the treasures they have kept from Edwardian and even Victorian days. Of course it is difficult for the elderly preacher to keep up with all the latest gadgetry— the overhead projectors, videotapes and so on; but I don't think this is expected of him, and sometimes I believe people actually prefer the more old-fashioned approach. I have always tried to keep visual-aids as uncomplicated as possible, for I believe they can come between speaker and hearer, and obscure rather than illuminate.

It is I think a great mistake for those of us who are old, and who still aspire to preach, to ape the methods of the next generation. We cannot do it nearly so well, and in any case it is unbecoming, like elderly men and women wandering about in jeans. People want us to 'be our age', and there are probably those who hear us who will secretly admit to themselves that 'having drunk old wine' they do not immediately want new; for, they say, 'the old is better' (Lk 5:39).

Counsel

When King Rehoboam succeeded Solomon his father, 'all Israel came to Shechem' to acclaim him. He could have had a wonderfully successful reign, and he began well by seeking the advice of the old men who had been his father's counsellors. 'And they said, "If today you are willing to serve this people, show yourself their servant now and speak kindly to them, and they will be your servants ever after'" (1 Kings 12:7, New English Bible). But he rejected this advice, and followed instead that of the young men who had grown up with him and who were to be his own counsellors. It was harsh, unsympathetic advice, and it resulted in civil war and the final division of the kingdom.

This is not to say that the advice of the elderly is always correct and that of younger men wrong; far from it. But so often the elderly, even if they err on the side of caution, can see history repeating itself, and how mistakes that have been made in the past, if they are not avoided, will lead to the same disasters as before. Of course it is possible to give advice in such a tactless and arrogant way that it has the very opposite effect to the one desired; and very often we need to adapt it to the temperament of the person seeking it. We are told that sometimes when Churchill's advisers saw that their counsel was meeting with resistance, they did not press the point, but left the seed severely alone to germinate in his mind. Some time later he would produce the fruit he had grown from this seed, and enthusiastically adopt it, because he had convinced himself that it was his own idea. People naturally shrink back from the cocksure and over-confident adviser. They like the sort of person who will approach the problem afresh, in the light of the prevailing circumstances, and whose attitude is not that of knowing the answers before the advice is sought, but thinking things through from the start. 'I wonder whether . . .' rather than 'I know what . . .' is the response of the man whose advice will be sought over and over again.

But to be a good adviser we must first become a good observer, for it is only upon a close observation of people and affairs that the right sort of advice can be based. It is probably true, as we have already remarked, that the spectator sees more of the game than the participator, but there are two kinds of spectator, those who attend and those who absorb. It is possible to have eyes 'and see not'. The elderly must train themselves to become good observers, to see, absorb and assess what is going on around them; to become 'critics' in the true sense of that word. We have already noted how Moses' father-in-law, Jethro, was able to do this. It did not escape his observant eye that his son-in-law was over-working, and his advice was based on an informed assessment. Once again, the relationship between critic and performer is a sensitive one, and it is interesting to see that Jethro's delicate and tactful handling of this matter caused absolutely no resentment or offence.

Sometimes it comes to light in the biography of a famous person, whom everyone regarded as completely independent and self-sufficient, that he or she had a guide, philosopher and friend tucked away somewhere in retirement; and it was to this person that they turned for encouragement and advice. When a new, brilliant but extremely young and untried Oxford don was appointed headmaster of my old school, one of the first things he did was to go to the most senior member of his staff, who had been there for more than thirty years, and say, 'Tell me all about Wellington.' His own willingness to learn would have been matched by the wisdom, experience and gentle tact of the man he approached. On the other hand, when someone I knew left a different kind of job after a brief unhappy period, an older friend, whose counsel he had sought, told me rather sadly that 'he did everything I advised him not to'.

It has been my privilege in life to serve on a large number of school governing councils. From time to time the cry goes up for the appointment of younger governors, those whose children are of school age, and who have first-hand experience of parenthood and adolescence. But such people are very hard to find, simply because at that age they are busy building their own careers and cannot spare the time; but, excellent though many of them would be, I am by no means convinced that at sixty-five or seventy people are incapable of new ideas and fresh thought, provided, as I have already said, one's powers of observation do not decline, and one's social antennae are kept alert and sensitive.

Those who have occupied public positions or held high office very often gain a well-deserved reputation as 'elder statesmen', and can use their retirement to exercise a very valuable influence. It is interesting, for example, to detect a certain mellowing in politicians when they are released from the verbal hooliganism of the House of Commons, and find themselves, perhaps, in the House of Lords. They acquire a new dignity and a less polemical outlook. They are prepared to admit that their opponents 'have a point', and they seem to be more open to argument.

To a certain extent this is true of all retired people. They can look at life and its problems from a more detached standpoint, and the advice they can give therefore is more objective. They are not so involved as they were, and no longer have a personal axe to grind. And there is nothing more mentally and spiritually stimulating for the elderly than to have their counsel sought by the young. It makes them think clearly and widely, it keeps them fresh and prevents intellectual vegetation; and it is very good for them when, as may well happen, they are led to see that their advice is not always for the best.

Correspondence

We must now turn to another way in which the elderly can make such a useful contribution, and this is by their correspondence. Letter-writing is in danger of becoming a lost art, overtaken and superseded by the telephone. In future we shall be offered 'The life and telephone conversations' instead of 'The life and letters' of famous people, as has been the case in the past. The trouble is that the telephone is much quicker and often cheaper than a letter, no matter how demanding and intrusive it may be.

But nothing can really take the place of the letter —the friendly little note on someone's birthday or other anniversary; the line of encouragement before an examination or interview; the longer, chatty letter to some distant friend or relation with all the latest news; and sometimes the sort of advice we have just been considering may best be conveyed by a letter rather than *viva voce*.

Letter-writing can be a wonderful ministry, and one for which the elderly are perhaps uniquely suited the more they find themselves confined to their own homes and unable to get about. I can still remember the enormous encouragement it was to me to receive letters from older Christian friends when I was at boarding school, and how my housemaster chided me on the size of my post.

A friend of mine, seriously handicapped by illness and an accident soon after his retirement, was able to get about very little. He saw it as his ministry to correspond with the young people he had known, and many of whom he had taught, scattered all over the world. No doubt his letter-writing, and the replies he received, stimulated prayer, and there is no way of knowing what an influence for good he exercised.

Of course, we can bore people with our letters, just as we can without meaning to, in our conversation. We can write too often or reply too quickly, our letters can be too long, too verbose and sometimes too illegible. I remember a piece of advice I was given before I started to work full time among young people, and that was to write as clearly and legibly as possible, especially to children. It was advice I frequently gave to my helpers at holiday camps and house parties. There is nothing more tedious than to have to decode a letter before you can read it. It makes all the difference, for example, if the letter 'e' is always opened, and easily distinguished from the letter 'i'; especially because some people have a habit of not dotting their 'i's', or only doing so three moves along. We get so used to the hastily scrawled letters we exchange with fellow-adults, that we sometimes forget how much more difficult it is for the very young. I make a great deal of use of the typewriter, and have done so for so long, that I find I can express myself more easily and clearly than in a hand-written letter. I don't think it need be or even appear to be any less personal, certainly not after a time.

There has never been a greater letter-writer than the apostle Paul. His letters have been called 'sent-sermons', and he used them to stimulate faith, to impart knowledge, to rebuke error, to convey news and to seek help. Letter-writing was possibly the most important and certainly the most permanent part of his ministry. He demonstrates, for all to see, the power of the letter, and that, 'Beneath the rule of men entirely great, the pen is mightier than the sword.'

7

The Contributions of Old Age—2

The other day I was travelling by train from King's Cross to Newcastle-upon-Tyne, when I was joined at Peterborough by six elderly women. They were on their way home, so they told me, from a 'whist-drive holiday' on the Norfolk coast. For the next hour or so there was a non-stop barrage of chatter and laughter. They all seemed to be talking at once at the top of their voices about themselves, their holiday, their homes, families and friends. When finally they left the train at Darlington to make a connection for Middlesbrough, one of them turned to me and said, 'Now you can be left in peace.' I smiled weakly to disguise my relief, and returned to my book. But on reflection I began to feel rather ashamed of myself.

Fellowship

To begin with, they were all so obviously making each other happy, and their camaraderie was so tangible, that it seemed almost churlish to resent the fact that they made it difficult for me to read. True, the thought of a 'whist-drive holiday' was not my idea of fun, even on the lovely Norfolk coast, but would I not have enjoyed that hour or so more if I had joined in their chatter, laughed with them, teased them (as the friendly ticket-inspector did) and—who knows?—perhaps imparted some good thing to them or received one myself? Looking back, I think I wasted the time trying to read against that barrage, and lost an opportunity of just being friendly.

Then, secondly, I reflected upon the fact that they obviously meant a great deal to each other, and were a very united, supportive little group; and I began to wonder whether we old people, in our desire not to appear older than we are, shrink from the company of other elderly people, and are apt to retreat into our own shells. There are many old people, it is true, whose circumstances oblige them to see too much of each other, because they all live together; but just as there is a certain solidarity among teenagers, so I think the elderly can derive comfort and strength from their contemporaries. I don't quite know how this would work out in my own case, living on my own as I do, and still working largely among younger people; but I think that experience on the train has deepened my sense of fellowship with people of my own age, shown me how much we need each other, and reminded me of what I should give and could receive.

Hospitality

Hospitality in Old Testament days was not just a custom, it was a fundamental duty, and a mark of faithfulness to God. The nomadic nature of life, the difficulties and dangers of travelling and the absence of inns and hostels made care for strangers and friends alike a basic social responsibility. Thus Job was able to say, 'The stranger did not lodge in the street: but I opened my doors to the traveller' (Job 31:32); and in Judges 19 we have a remarkable example of the lengths to which an unnamed 'old man' was prepared to go to protect his visitors against those who tried to abuse his hospitality towards them.

Hospitality is something which old age gives us a special opportunity to provide, and the New Testament is full of exhortations to us to do so. We are to 'show' it, to 'love' it and to 'give ourselves to' it. Two classes of people are particularly mentioned: widows and bishops. Widows who had reached the age of sixty were allowed to qualify for a supplementary benefit from the church, but only if they had 'given hospitality' (1 Tim 5:9-10); while both Timothy (1 Tim 3:2) and Titus (Tit 1:8) were instructed that candidates for the episcopacy must have a good 'A' level in hospitality.

For many years I was chaplain to the then Bishop of Rochester, Dr Christopher Chavasse, and I used to attend his ordination retreats at Bishopscourt as a kind of adjutant. He was a true 'Father in God', and it was his wish that all ordinands should feel that they were not just coming into a diocese, but into a family. The hospitality which he and Mrs Chavasse provided was amazing, and even at the height of the war all meals were taken in their own dining-room, with perhaps as many as sixteen round the table. And not for him the silent meals we heard about in other dioceses, where, as he put it, 'You have to wink for the pepper.' They were essentially times of fellowship, with talk and laughter flowing free. On occasion we would be joined by Noel Chavasse, the bishop's son and 'Monty's' aide-de-camp who would invite himself, as he put it, to 'jolly the thing along'. It needed very little jollying, though for safety's sake I was usually placed next to him to act as a shock absorber for some of his less clerical stories. I would see Mrs Chavasse looking anxiously from one end of the table, and the bishop straining his ears from the other. Small wonder they are both remembered with such affection!

All my working life I have been the recipient of other people's hospitality. Having a job which at one time meant spending up to half the nights of the year away from home, I have been overwhelmed by the care and kindness of Christian people, as I was told I would be when I started, by someone who had been in the same sort of work for many years before me.

It is one of my regrets that I have so far been able to do so little in return. Being a bachelor and living alone do not make it easy, especially as I still travel a good deal, particularly at weekends. But as I begin to slow up a bit, and spend more time at home, I am hoping that I may be able to do something to repay the hospitality I have enjoyed.

It is, as I have said, a form of service which is peculiarly appropriate for the elderly and retired to provide, but it must not be thought that it is all giving on their part, and there is nothing to be gained. The writer to the Hebrews says this: 'Remember to show hospitality. There are some who, by so doing, have entertained angels without knowing it' (Heb 13:2, New English Bible). We all know what it is to take leave of a guest with genuine sadness, because they have so enriched us with their presence.

Prayer

Perhaps the most important thing the elderly can do is to pray—to intercede for the needs of others; but having said that, I find it quite the hardest thing to do. I find it fairly easy to advise, to write letters and to be a friend; but when it comes to prayer, I am ashamed how difficult I find it— though perhaps that is the measure of its value and importance.

The maddening thing is that we know this in theory. We know that 'More things are wrought by prayer than this world dreams of,' but we jib at the second part of Tennyson's famous quotation, 'Therefore let thy voice rise like a fountain for me night and day.' Yet the elderly have more time for prayer than anyone else, and I know how marvellously some old people make use of this secret weapon. They hold a very high rank in what has been called 'The Royal Prayer Force'. My mother used to tell me what a debt my sisters, brother and I owed to her mother, our grandmother; and I can well believe that she used much of her time, spent in a wheelchair, because she was a cripple, in prayer for others.

Perhaps this is a good moment to digress slightly

and consider just how important the prayers and spiritual influence of old people can be to the next generation but one. Parents who want to see their children, in the words of the old Prayer Book, 'Christianly and virtuously brought up' face a daunting responsibility, and need all the prayer and help they can receive.

I always think that one of the most heartbreaking experiences of Christian parents must be to watch their children, on whom they have lavished infinite care and much prayer, abandon the faith they have been taught, and wander off into the spiritual wilderness. It was this among other things that cast a shadow over Samuel's closing years, for we read that 'When Samuel grew old, he made his sons judges in Israel. . . . But they did not follow their father's example; they were interested only in making money, so they accepted bribes and did not decide cases honestly' (1 Sam 8:1-3, GNB).

I remember once scandalizing the wife of an archdeacon when I was a young man, by saying that I would rather not have a child at all than have one if I knew in advance that he or she would never become a Christian. I think I still feel the same, but of course we cannot know in advance, and Christian parents quite rightly take a calculated step of faith when they decide to have a family. But it is one of the hazards of parenthood, a risk, if we may say so, that God himself took when he created man, that children may turn away from the faith they have been taught from childhood. Parents will cling wistfully to some early sign of commitment, long since overlaid, and hope that the seed sown then will eventually bear fruit. I believe it is here that the help of Christian grandparents can often be enlisted, and their prayers can turn the tide.

But as I look around the families of my innumerable Christian friends, I am bound to say that there is an enormous amount of cause for praise to God, and despite some disappointments, I think they have been more successful in the Christian upbringing of their children than the previous generation was.

There is of course no formula for the Christian upbringing of children, and after all we are reminded that the grace of God which leads to the new birth is 'not of blood, nor of the will of the flesh, nor of the will of man, but of God' (Jn 1:13). In other words, it cannot be inherited, contrived or induced. From first to last it is a miracle. But like all miracles there is a part that man must play. It was not the water in the well that Jesus turned into wine at Cana of Galilee, but the water that had been collected by the servants in the waterpots.

> Fill the water-pots with water,
> Fill them to the very brim;
> Do exactly as he tells you,
> Leave the miracle to him.

But what are the conditions which parents must fulfil and the mistakes they must try to avoid?

I often look back to my own childhood with immense gratitude to my own parents. All four of their children grew up to be committed Christians, and now it has gone on into the next generation. By modern standards I suppose our upbringing would have been considered rather strict. Sunday, for example, was spent very quietly. We didn't play games, we wore suits, we went to church— usually twice—we read what were called 'Sunday books', we made a sort of ritual tour of the garden and greenhouses and we went for walks. But I don't remember being bored, and my recollections of those quiet days are happy ones. I think perhaps it was because Sunday was different. Golf and tennis, cricket and hockey which among other things filled the rest of the week were laid aside for one day, and the change was welcome. *O tempora O mores!* I am not suggesting that I have followed that pattern all my life, or that it would be acceptable in Christian families today.

That it did not put us off, as it might be expected to do today, was partly due to the fact that it was in keeping with the pattern of Christian life which existed before the war. It would have been as unthinkable for me not to wear a suit on Sundays as it is for the idea to occur to the young Christian of today. But looking more deeply, I think the happiness of my home life lay in the love and laughter that prevailed, the undercurrent of Christian faith and the more overt acceptance, as a family, of Christian standards. It was the very opposite of 'pi'. We rarely if ever talked religion at meals, and my father, unless he happened to be wearing a dog-collar, was just about the last person you would have suspected of being a parson.

Perhaps all Christian parents ought to read Edmund Gosse's book *Father and Son*. It tells the true story of how the son, Sir Edmund Gosse, as he became, reacted against the rigidly narrow and legalistic religion of his father, and is an object lesson in how not to bring up a child. I must hasten to add that never in real life have I met the sort of home described there; but Sir Edmund Gosse was born in 1849.

There are however two mistakes which I think Christian parents need to avoid. The first is to try to give their children too much too soon. There are of course certain fundamental things that a child should see or learn: that it is the living presence of Jesus Christ and faith in him that gives the home its love and peace and joy; and that there is a very definite difference between right and wrong.

As to the first, I remember once a parent saying to me apropos one of my camps which his son had attended, 'He learnt to equate religion and joy.' I think this is important. If Sunday is the happiest day of the week, if Sunday books are the best, if there is 'laughter learnt of friends and gentleness in hearts at peace', then children are going to catch the infection of their parents' faith; and as the old cliché has it, 'true religion is caught, not taught'.

Dick Hudson Pope, to whose skill as a children's evangelist I owe so much, always used to say, 'Don't underrate the under-eights,' meaning that they would often surprise you with how much they could absorb and understand. But he also made the charmingly heretical remark that he thought children of that age were saved by works rather than by faith. I know exactly what he meant. The law must come first, for it is our schoolmaster to lead us to Christ. An understanding of what is right and wrong must precede an understanding of the need for forgiveness. It has been said that a child's moral education comes in three stages: *I must*, when it does what it is told often for no better reason than 'Because I say so'; *I ought*, when a sense of duty and indebtedness takes over, and it begins to see for itself the difference between right and wrong; and *I want*, when love for parents, for neighbours and above all for God becomes the mainspring and the motive of moral behaviour.

It is possible for parents, in their enthusiasm to see a child put his trust in Christ, to put the cart before the horse, and not to lay the solid foundations on which any profession of commitment must be built. When parents tell me that their child aged six has given his heart to Christ, I am afraid I am inclined to say, 'Fancy!' because I fear it may have been an artificially induced decision. When a man of fifty tells me that he was only six when he took that step, then I say 'Super!' In other words, I believe most firmly in child-conversion, but I am fearful of a response which may simply be due to parental pressure.

Perhaps one of the most difficult things Christian parents have to do is to be willing for their own spiritual influence to be supplanted at an early age by that of someone outside the family— a teacher, perhaps, or a godparent, or holiday friend. In my own case I always admired the wisdom of my parents who felt this to be my need, and encouraged me at the appropriate age to attend a Christian house party in the holidays. It was not that what they had taught me was wasted; far from it, for the new experience I gained away from home was made all the more understandable and enduring by what I had absorbed, often unconsciously, at home.

But there are some parents who go to the opposite extreme. In their anxiety not to pressurize their children, they do too little too late. The home is too liberal, too permissive, too unstructured. The result is that the child grows up without the necessary moral and spiritual scaffolding, and the challenge of Christ, when it comes later in life, meets him at a time when he has slipped too far into easy-going worldliness and indifference.

It is very easy for a bachelor like me to pontificate on these matters. I have never had to deal with the problem, but in the belief that the spectator sometimes sees most of the game, I have been able to observe how things are done in the countless Christian homes in which I have stayed. I can only say that in the vast majority of cases I have been most favourably impressed at the balance that Christian parents have achieved, and where there have been disappointments, they are not always obviously traceable to the sort of mistakes I have outlined above.

I think there are certain occupations which make it harder for some parents than for others. The clergy, for example, or the heads of boarding schools cannot easily separate their homes from their work. They cannot leave their problems on their desk as other people can, and these are apt to invade the life of the family. This can lead to children feeling that they are being 'shared' with parishioners or pupils, and are to that extent deprived. In some ways a father with a whole week-end to spend at home, even if he is away for much of the week, can give his children more undivided attention.

But at the same time I think it is nonsense, as I have heard it said, that the children of clergy tend to grow up irreligious. Indeed, I think it would hardly be possible to express the opposite of the truth more precisely; for there are probably few careers, except perhaps the army, which run in families more than that of the Christian ministry.

In my own case we could have fielded an eleven of fairly close clerical relations.

I sometimes wonder whether the church authorities pay as much attention as they should to St Paul's injunction concerning the families of those whom they think of appointing as bishops—that they should 'rule' their own house well, 'having [their] children in subjection with all gravity; (for if a man know not how to rule his own house, how shall he take care of the church of God?)' (1 Tim 3:4–5). There are few more powerful or eloquent witnesses in the world today than a truly united Christian home.

All this has taken us some distance from the prayers of grandparents for their grandchildren, but I hope it has underlined the importance of such prayers. I am a great believer in 'Christian dynasties', and have lived long enough to see them run to the third and even fourth generation. The elderly vicar (three times my own age) whom I served for three or four years as a curate, was converted as a schoolboy in 1882 during a visit of D.L. Moody to his home county of Devon. If he had lived, he would now be about 115, and it would have rejoiced his heart (as indeed I believe it does) to see his great-grandchildren launching out into Christian service; and they, I feel sure, thank God that his prayers have been answered 'from one generation to another'.

As we bear in mind the problems that Christian parents have, and how often they feel unqualified to deal with them, it should inspire those of us who belong to a previous generation to pray all the harder. We can well imagine how fervently Lois prayed for Timothy (2 Tim 1:5) and we hope she had the joy of seeing him brought to the Lord and launched out into Christian service. I have eleven nephews and nieces and I try to pray for them regularly. They may be beyond the range of my influence in other ways, but in prayer we have a mysterious secret weapon at our disposal, and it is certainly a joy to know how many of them are beginning to found Christian families in their turn. We shall probably never know the mechanics of prayer, how it enables God to work in the world, how far it restrains the power of Satan, and whether or not there is actually some way in which spiritual strength is transferred. It was Archbishop William Temple who used to say that the one thing about prayer of which he was certain was that when he stopped praying coincidences stopped happening.

In Ralph Rickett's book, *Bid the world good-night* there is a delightful contribution by Daphne du Maurier. She tells of an old lady named 'Shirley' aged eighty-two, blind and very unsteady on her legs, but a devout Christian. There seemed to be very little that she could do, but she did not want just to sit around all day listening to the radio, so she 'made a great plan' to think of and pray for all the sick and unhappy people in the world. 'It will work like my radio here,' she explained to Daphne du Maurier, 'the thought, the prayer, will somehow reach them. So, my dear, just make a list of anyone you know who is ill or miserable, and when you next come, tell me their names, and I'll add them to the number.'

Samuel regarded failure to pray as a sin (1 Sam 12:23). After reproaching the people for their wickedness (in this case in asking for a king), he said to them, 'God forbid that I should sin against the Lord in ceasing to pray for you.' In other words, 'My failure, my sin, may not have been what you have done, but it would be in ceasing to pray for you all the time.' And Paul, to judge by his incessant prayer for the churches in his care, would no doubt have felt and said the same.

I said that the difficulty we find in praying is perhaps the measure of its importance. If it really is the force we believe it to be, then we can be sure that Satan will do all in his power to prevent it, and we need resolution and determination to thwart him. We are all familiar with the need for regular times of prayer, but perhaps one or two other suggestions may help.

As well as a list, which I find essential, I find it quite helpful to have a few photographs on the wall in front of me as I pray, so that I can picture the people concerned in my mind. Again, there is an art, which I can't pretend to have mastered, of turning our thoughts about people into prayers. I think that is what Paul must have meant when he said in his letter to the Philippians, 'I thank my God upon every remembrance [or mention] of you' (Phil 1:3). Some elderly people have learnt how to pray at night, when they find it hard to sleep, and like David know how to use what he called 'the night watches' (Ps 63:6); while others again are able to associate certain places, landmarks, trees and so on with people, so that as they pass them they are reminded of the one for whom they should pray.

Life may not exactly begin at sixty, but no one, and certainly no Christian, has the right to imagine that its purpose and value end at that age; for there is an enormously rich contribution which the elderly can make to society at large. If overnight everyone over the age of sixty were liquidated, the state would no doubt save a very great deal of money, but in countless other ways it would be enormously impoverished, not least, as we shall see in the next chapter, because God seems sometimes to hold people back, so that they only really take off and begin their greatest work when all their contemporaries have retired.

Some Grand Old People

At the age of eighty-three, Wesley was piqued to discover that he could not write for more than fifteen hours a day without hurting his eyes; and at the age of eighty-six, he was ashamed to admit that he could not preach more than twice a day. In his eighty-sixth year he preached in every county in England and Wales, and often rode thirty to fifty miles a day.

'To what cause can I impute this?' he asked himself. 'First to the power of God, fitting me to the work to which I am called; and next to the prayers of his children. Then may I also impute it to these inferior means:

1. My constant exercise and change of air.
2. My never having lost a night's sleep, sick or well, on land or at sea.
3. My having slept at command, whether day or night.
4. My having risen constantly at 4 am for about sixty years.
5. My constant preaching at 5 am for above fifty years.

6. My having so little pain, sorrow or anxious care in
   life.'

Polycarp, Bishop of Smyrna and friend of the apostle
John, was condemned to death as a Christian at the age
of eighty-six. Given the chance to renounce Christ, he
replied, 'Eighty and six years have I served him and he
never did me any injury. How then can I blaspheme my
King and my Saviour?'

But none of these things move me, neither count I my
life dear unto myself, so that I might finish my course
with joy, and the ministry, which I have received of the
Lord Jesus, to testify the gospel of the grace of God.

Paul (Acts 20:24)

8

Some Grand Old People

In Old Testament days longevity was regarded as a
mark of divine approval and a reward for a right-
eous life (Ex 20:12; Prov 3:1-2), and to ask for
'length of days' for oneself and one's descendants
was a natural and proper thing to do. We can
understand why this should be so at a time when
the full light of the resurrection had not yet
dawned upon people, and when ideas about the
life to come were at best very shadowy and vague.
As David rather sadly put it in a time of sickness,
'For in death there is no remembrance of thee: in
the grave who shall give thee thanks?' (Ps 6:5).

It is obvious from this that very old people were
the élite of society, and earned very great respect.
They, rather than the rich or mighty, were the true
aristocrats, because God had bestowed upon them
the accolade of old age. We have an example of this
in the very deferential way in which Pharaoh received Jacob, and allowed him to give him his blessing. Today it would be the other way round.

Jacob's answer to the question 'How old are you' (or, as we might say, 'What rank do you hold?') had an almost ceremonial, ritualistic ring about it: 'The days of the years of my pilgrimage are an hundred and thirty years: few and evil have the days of the years of my life been, and have not attained unto the days of the years of the life of my fathers in the days of their pilgrimage' (Gen 47:9). It is almost as if he were saying, 'I should have been worthy of a much longer life still.'

But since the coming of Christ, and the opening of the gates of heaven to all believers, we accept the fact that a long life is not to be equated with any special merit or virtue. Two world wars have proved that, if proof were necessary, and reminded us that death is no respecter of persons. It 'lays its icy hands on kings' as it does upon everyone else. We have grown accustomed too to the fact that very often small is beautiful, for as Ben Jonson put it in the Pindaric ode he wrote in honour of Sir H. Morison:

> It is not growing like a tree
> In bulk, doth make man better be;
> Nor standing long an oak, three hundred year,
> To fall a log at last, dry, bald and sere.
> A lily of a day
> Is fairer far in May,
> Although it fall and die that night;
> It was the plant and flower of light.
> In small proportions we just beauties see
> And in short measures, life may perfect be.

I believe it is fruitless to speculate as to the reasons why some of the noblest and most useful lives are cut off at the very height of their power. It has always been so. No doubt there have been 'saints, apostles, prophets, martyrs' 'of whom the world was not worthy' (Heb 11:38), and whom God took to be with himself because they were better off out of it, illustrating perhaps the old pagan belief that 'whom the gods love die young'. But I think these are the exception.

Every now and then the mystery is brought sharply into focus as it has been recently with the death of David Watson, perhaps the most widely used of all evangelists in this country since the war. The same questions were asked about a hundred years ago when Henry Drummond died at the age of forty-five. His influence from the age of twenty-three, when D.L. Moody made him responsible for his student work, had been enormous. His biographer, George Adam Smith, while he knew that hundreds had gone to him for help, 'was prepared neither for the quality nor for the extent of influence which his correspondence reveals. . . . Men and women sought him who were of every rank of life and of almost every nation under the sun.' And yet, when it seemed that he was at the zenith of his power, he was smitten with an incurable disease. There is no answer that I can see to mysterious riddles of this sort. We must content ourselves in believing that it will be given to us when the time is ripe, when we no longer see things reflected in a dim and distorted mirror, but clearly and face to face.

But our concern in this chapter is with those whose work and influence extended far beyond the age at which most people retire, and the Bible and history are full of examples of those of whom the Bible says, 'They shall still bring forth fruit in old age' (Ps 92:14). Consider, for instance, this list of modern statesmen with the age in brackets at which they finally surrendered office: Adenauer (77), Ben Gurion (77), Churchill (80), Gandhi (79), Smuts (78), Haile Selassie (83), De Gaulle (78). We could extend this list almost indefinitely if we went behind the iron curtain; and when we add to it those who have done some of their best work in science, art, literature and so on after the age of sixty-five, those approaching that age should be encouraged to realize what an effective influence they can have in later years.

Many a clergyman has held important office until well into his seventies and even eighties; and it is only recently that it has become the practice for archbishops to retire; they used to die in harness. John Wesley spent his seventy-fifth birthday in Ireland. Sunday, June 28th, 1788 found him in the midst of a three-and-a-half month tour of the island, preaching almost every day, visiting, writing, reading and travelling. 'I am today seventy-five years old,' he wrote in his journal, 'and I do not find myself, blessed be God, any weaker than I was at five-and-twenty. This also hath God wrought. All this week I visited as many as I could, and endeavoured to confirm their love to each other; and I have not known the Society for many years so united as it is now.'

There are many men and women in the Bible who lived to be an exceptional age, and from whose experience, whether it was successful or not, we may learn a lot about how to 'bring forth fruit in old age'. We have already noted *Jacob*, and the dignity and humility he retained to the end. *Eli* lived to be ninety-eight, and still exercised supervision over the ark of God. But his powers were failing rapidly, and he had largely lost his grip, when he died of a broken heart, having heard that the ark of the Lord had been captured and of the apostasy of his two sons, Hophni and Phineas. 'Ichabod' ('the glory has departed') was not only a fitting name for his grandson, but a sad commentary on the state of the nation. Perhaps he ought to have retired years before, but was there anyone to take his place? And at least in his closing years he was able to guide the first steps of the boy Samuel (1 Sam 3 and 4). *Barzillai* was a fine old aristocrat from Gilead who revered and supported David. As a reward for his loyalty and hospitality, David tried to persuade him to return with him to court, when the rebellion was over. But with touching humility Barzillai pleaded old age (he was eighty) and asked to be allowed to return home. 'Why should I be a burden to the king?' he asked, unselfish to the last (2 Sam 17:27; 19:32, 39; 21:8). *David* himself lived to be over seventy, though it is not surprising that his hectic, adventurous life had worn him out, and we read that he was 'stricken with years' and 'gat no heat' (1 Kings 1:1). But he seems to have remained mentally alert to the end, and is to be greatly commended for the foresight he showed in preparing and equipping his son, Solomon, and establishing him in his place upon the throne.

Turning to the New Testament, it is interesting to note that two of the first people to acknowledge Jesus as Lord were *Simeon* and *Anna* whose long lives of devoted service were at the end rewarded by this revelation (Lk 2:25–38). *Paul*, although he probably did not live to be seventy, referred to himself as 'Paul the aged' (Philem 9), prematurely worn out, no doubt, through all he had done and suffered for his Master. For him there was no comfortable retirement or ample pension. Only at the last did he take 'the leave that knows no ending'. Until then he was always in action, and more truthfully than most, he was able to say, 'I will not cease from mental fight, nor shall my sword sleep in my hand. . . .'

Doubtless there are others whom we could mention, but our chief concern in this chapter is with those who would probably tell us that their greatest work was achieved long after the age when they might reasonably have expected to take honourable retirement; who seem in fact to have been held back for some special purpose, and then given almost superhuman strength to cope with the challenge and demands with which they found themselves confronted. In other words, if they had died before the normal retiring age, they might easily have passed into almost complete oblivion.

The most striking and obvious example in modern times of what I mean is of course Sir Winston Churchill. In the early 1930s he was written off as a brilliant and erratic failure like his father before him. The Labour Party regarded him as an implacable enemy, the Liberals as a renegade, while to the Conservatives he was a heretic over India and rearmament. It looked as if 'The wilderness years' could never end. And then came the war. Six months after his sixty-fifth birthday he became Prime Minister, and continued in and out of office until he was eighty. It was difficult not to believe that he had been raised up in the good providence of God for the crisis which faced this country; and the words spoken to Esther by her uncle, Mordecai, when she found herself uniquely placed to save the lives of her countrymen and women, the Jews, applied most forcibly to him: 'Who knoweth whether thou art come to the kingdom for such a time as this?' (Esther 4:14).

The Bible contains at least three examples of the same thing, men whose life's work began at the age when most people are bringing theirs to an end; men who, if God had not called them out of retirement and even obscurity might never have been heard of, and who would have left a great work undone.

Abraham

At seventy-five Abraham could reasonably have looked forward to a quiet old age, but God had very different plans for him. He was called to be the founding father of a great nation, and to leave his home in Ur in Chaldea for the life of a nomad and a stranger. It is difficult enough at that age to leave one home for another, and those who are obliged to do so make sure they know exactly where they are going before they move. But it was not like that with Abraham, 'he went out, not knowing where he was going' (Heb 11:8, Revised Standard Version) in complete obedience and trust in God to guide him; and in doing so he set a marvellous example for all to follow, young and old.

The elderly must never assume that God may not call them to some new adventure or enterprise for himself. As Christians, as soldiers of the cross, we never retire. God reserves the right to call us up at any time for any purpose.

Faith and obedience were the hallmarks of Abraham's life and the secrets of his great success.

He trusted God when he was asked to do something which was beyond his reason to understand; and he obeyed when what he was asked to do must have been against his wishes. 'Trust and obey' are the first steps in the Christian life, and also the last. It would be the duty of a soldier in the old days, when he was on the reserve, to keep his sword sharp and bright. Our sword must be treated like that, and one edge is called 'trust' and the other 'obey'. I remember some years ago, when I thought I had probably played my last game of cricket, giving away my equipment to some younger friends. Once or twice since then I have regretted it. A challenge, albeit a very minor one, has come my way, and I have been unprepared to meet it.

'Be prepared', the motto of the Boy Scout movement, is a very sound one for Christians too; and it is interesting to note how often the words, 'I am ready', spring to the lips of Paul. Like Abraham, he too was ready for service and ready for sacrifice. At seventy-five Abraham was as alert and ready to answer God's call as he had been at twenty-five. That, it seems to me, is the lesson he has to teach us today.

Moses

The first eighty years of Moses' life were something of a disaster. Desperately anxious to help his oppressed fellow countrymen in their plight, he resorted to violence, was forced to leave the country, and spent the best years of his life as an exile and refugee. But all this time, though he did not know it, God was quietly preparing him for the call which finally came at the age of eighty. His deep compassion for his compatriots was being tempered by wisdom, and his stamina by the tough, demanding life of a desert shepherd (Ex 2).

Moses was not without his shortcomings. He was inclined to be impatient, and his hot temper more than once got him into trouble. He found it difficult to delegate to others, and tried to do everything himself, until he listened to the advice of his father-in-law, Jethro (Ex 18). And his diffidence at one point almost exhausted God's patience, if we may put it like that (Ex 3).

It was not altogether surprising. To challenge the authority of a capricious and unpredictable tyrant like Pharaoh and then to prepare and conduct one of the greatest military operations in history would have daunted a man half his age. But of course Moses was asking the wrong question. It was not 'Who am I . . .?' that mattered, but 'Who are you?' For he was not called upon to undertake this task in his own strength, but in that which God supplied; and for the next forty years, in circumstances of the utmost hardship, and often torn by internal strife and dissension, he was to prove the truth of Paul's famous remark, 'my strength is made perfect in weakness' (2 Cor 12:9). The result was that Moses emerged as one of the greatest leaders in history, admired by people like Churchill, who has an essay about him in *Thoughts and Adventures,* and even by Field Marshal Montgomery, who dubbed him 'a great guy'.

Once again, as in the case of Abraham, the lesson for us is clear. It may be that God will call us to some major task in old age, for which he has been preparing us during years past. If so, we can be sure that he will equip us with the necessary strength, for God's commands are God's enablings. When it comes to spiritual stamina old age should not put us at a disadvantage, for God is no respecter of persons. Indeed, almost the reverse, for we are told that 'Even the youths shall faint and be weary, and the young men shall utterly fall: but they that wait upon the Lord shall renew their strength; they shall mount up with wings as eagles, they shall run, and not be weary; and they shall walk, and not faint' (Is 40:30-31). In Moses' case we are told that at the incredible age of one hundred and twenty 'his eye was not dim, nor his natural force abated' (Deut 34:7), but even those whose physical powers are not as great as his may continue to be used by God just so long as they allow his strength to be made perfect in their own weakness.

Daniel

I have always regarded Daniel as one of the most fascinating characters in the Old Testament. Like Joseph, many years before him, he found himself in a foreign country—an exile and a prisoner of war; and yet he made himself so acceptable and indispensable that he rose to be Prime Minister in the country of his adoption. He and Joseph both illustrate the remarkable gift of the Jews throughout history for self-adaptation and talent and the ability to rise to the top in politics, industry, finance, science and art.

Daniel and his friends were obviously chosen for their princely background and potential, and they quickly proved their worth. Daniel's God-given gift for interpreting dreams brought him to the notice of King Nebuchadnezzar. On the first occasion the interpretation was favourable (Dan 2), and he was rewarded with gifts and great responsibility. It is characteristic of him that he did not forget his friends, whose prayers he had sought, and they too were promoted.

Some years later the king had another dream, and this time the interpretation was very unfavourable, for it foretold his insanity which took the form of the disease known as lycanthropy, when a man assumes the manners and characteristics of a wolf. There is no reason to suppose that this melancholy prediction put Daniel out of favour, for the king made a complete recovery, and his last recorded words reveal a touching humility—'Now I Nebuchadnezzar praise and extol and honour the king of heaven . . . those that walk in pride he is able to abase' (Dan 4:37).

Some time after these events it is likely that Daniel retired and slipped into obscurity. We next hear of him in the year 539 B.C. when he must have been about eighty. The new king, Belshazzar, was holding a great pagan feast, when there appeared the hand of a man writing on the wall. Terrified by what he saw, and unable to obtain any help from his own magicians, he was advised to send for Daniel.

It must have needed courage to impart bad news to Nebuchadnezzar, but Daniel seems to have established a very friendly relationship with that king. It was a very different matter with his successor, for there was no fear of God in his eyes, and Daniel must have noticed that the sacred vessels from his beloved temple were being used for this drunken orgy (Dan 5). But he did not hesitate for a moment.

He bluntly refused the king's offer of promotion, and before interpreting the writing, and in front of the assembled company, he preached the most terrific sermon, ending with the words, 'the God in whose hand thy breath is, and whose are all thy ways, hast thou not glorified' (Dan 5:23). Then followed the interpretation of the mysterious writing: 'Your kingdom is finished . . . you are weighed and found wanting . . . your kingdom is divided and given to the Medes and Persians.' That very night Darius invaded Babylon, and Belshazzar was slain.

We talk much about the mellowing effect of old age, the more careful choice of words, the greater tact and wisdom; and no doubt much of this process is good and desirable. But there was not much sign of it in Daniel's indictment of the king who must have felt like Mary Stuart listening to one of John Knox's famous diatribes in 1567, or James I of England and VI of Scotland squirming beneath a sermon based on James 1:6. Daniel's courage was immense. There was no apology, no gentle introduction, no attempt to soften the bad news. No wonder that some time later he was trapped by his jealous contemporaries and thrown into the lion's den! No wonder too that the lions left him severely alone! They didn't relish a diet of backbone and guts, as someone has said.

Once again, I find a lesson for myself in old age. Of course it is right that we should mellow. There ought to be a greater understanding and sympathy in the elderly than there is in the young, a greater tolerance and readiness to forgive. We have made too many mistakes ourselves to look without compassion upon those of a younger generation. It is right and proper, too, for the young to see issues clearly in black and white, for, as an experienced missionary said to me when I was a student at Cambridge, 'If you are not dogmatic at twenty you are not anywhere at forty.'

And that is the danger we have to guard against as we get older. The line which divides what is mellow from what is mouldy is a very narrow one, and it is very easy for the elderly to begin to see doctrinal truths and moral behaviour in pastel shades rather than in strong, primary colours. It does not matter, we are told, whether the virgin birth or the resurrection actually took place, it is what they signify that counts; and as to morals, why there is nothing either good or bad but circumstances make it so; and nice, glossy words are found for what the Bible calls sin. It probably started in Germany where 'murder' became 'liquidation' or 'the final solution'. So we don't talk about 'stealing', we prefer 'nicking', or 'lifting' or even 'borrowing'. We don't 'commit adultery', we just 'have an affair'. We never 'lie', we simply 'exaggerate'. But surely, however old we grow, we must be as firm and unequivocal as ever on fundamental doctrines and principles.

It was here that Daniel set us such a splendid example. He called a spade a spade. He didn't go to the other extreme and cause offence by calling it 'a b . . . y shovel', but he could say with the South African poet, Mungo Campbell:

> I would go stark, and let my meanings show
> Clear as a milk white feather in a crow,
> Or a black stallion in a field of snow.

The Bible tells us that 'them that honour me I will honour' (1 Sam 2:30), and it must have come as something of a surprise to Daniel that the king actually kept his word in spite of the horrific tidings he had just received. His last act was to promote Daniel to be the third ruler in the kingdom (Belshazzar himself was only Prince Regent) and clothe him with the robes of office. Thus it was that Darius found him, confirmed the appointment, and made him his chief minister.

The old hymn, 'Dare to be Daniel, dare to stand alone, dare to have a purpose firm, dare to make it known,' is one which is usually associated with children, and of course if we read the whole story, we would see that from the very earliest days Daniel took an uncompromising stand for the Lord. But the supreme test came, not to a boy in his early teens, not to a man at the height of his power, but to a frail and elderly man of eighty.

It could well be that for some of his elderly servants, continuing along the even tenor of the route they have prepared for themselves, God has strange and unexpected plans. He may want us to move off at right angles to the direction we are following, and to face some altogether different challenge and responsibility. If such a call should come, let us remind ourselves of the lessons these three Old Testament heroes have taught us, and pray for Abraham's faith, Moses' strength and Daniel's courage.

The Next Stage

A man once read his own obituary notice in the papers, and immediately rang up his best friend to re-assure him. 'Have you seen the notice of my death in *The Times*'? he asked. 'No,' replied his friend, 'where are you ringing from?'

And when the Emperor Franz-Joseph died in the middle of World War I it was feared an immediate announcement would demoralize the people. It was therefore stated that 'he had gone away to an undisclosed destination.'

> There is no death! What seems so is transition;
> This mortal breath
> Is but a suburb of the life Elysian,
> Whose portal we call death.
>
> *Longfellow*

Old men go to death and death comes to young men.

Bacon

Death is not a full stop, but only a comma in the story of life.

Time is the chrysalis of eternity.

Those who love God never meet for the last time.

W.G. Elmslie

'I cannot think what we shall do in heaven,' said Luther, 'no change, no work, no eating, no drink, nothing to do.'
'Yes,' said Melanchthon, 'Lord, show us the Father and it sufficeth us.'
'Why, of course,' replied Luther, 'that sight will give us quite enough to do.'

'Let not your heart be troubled: you believe in God, believe also in me. In my Father's house are many mansions: if it were not so, I would have told you. I go to prepare a place for you.'

Jn 14:1-2

9

The Next Stage

One of the curious things that strikes you as you grow old is the realization that people are talking about and planning things which you will never live to see. It is a strange sensation when it dawns on you for the first time that some new motorway or perhaps the Channel Tunnel will not be completed during your lifetime; and it brings home what I suppose all of us try subconsciously to postpone, the quiet, inexorable approach of death.

It is curious, too, that death, the one inescapable 'fact of life', is the last thing we talk about. It was not always so. A hundred years ago and more, sex was the taboo subject, but now it is death. In Victorian families, often running well into double figures, there were nearly always one or two who did not survive infancy. Therefore the subject could not be avoided. The average age to which people lived was about half what it is today, simply because illnesses like diphtheria and typhoid and tuberculosis carried off so many young people, and have today been practically eliminated. In Haworth Parish Church there is a tablet to the Brontë family, and it reminds us that all of them pre-deceased and were buried by the father.

It was a subject which was also dear to the heart of Victorian authors. It is true that they very often sentimentalized it, and we only have to look at some of the tombstones in our graveyards to see the extravagant way in which it was frequently des-cribed. But if they sentimentalized it, we today are in danger of trivializing it. The Victorians when they died were 'called home', or 'called to higher service', whereas we tend to 'kick the bucket' or 'pack up'.

But there is a more serious reason why it is a subject to be avoided today. The faith and hope with which our forefathers viewed the approach of death have now been abandoned by so many people. An increasing number of people believe we are just snuffed out at death, like a candle, and for this reason prefer not to think about the matter until they are forced to do so.

It is not just unthinking or unreflective people who hold this view, for it is shared by some of the deepest-thinking modern philosophers. The Sad-ducees in Jesus' day were no fools, but they did not believe in a resurrection (Mk 12:18), and today's sceptics are their successors. 'Man,' they argue, 'hates the idea of total extinction and so he has invented an after-life to give himself something to cling to.' This view was well expressed by that charming but atheistic poet Rupert Brooke in a mischievous little poem called 'Heaven'. He im-agines fish discussing the prospect of immortality in their stream or pond:

> Fish say they have their pool and pond,
> But is there anything beyond?
> This life cannot be all, they swear,
> For how unpleasant if it were!
> But somewhere, beyond space and time,
> Is wetter water, slimier slime,
> And there, fish say, there swimmeth one
> Who swam ere waters were begun . . .

How does the Christian answer criticisms and disbelief of this sort? I don't think we can deal with the after-life in isolation. It is just one part of the supernatural view of the world. If we believe that there is a God, then it is unthinkable that he has not made us for ultimate fellowship with himself, and that this will be experienced after physical death. There is in most people an instinct, something deeper than wishful-thinking, that tells them that 'this life cannot be all' there is. Some would even argue that psychic research and a study of the para-normal provide them with scientific proof of life after death, but this is taking us perilously close to an area which the Christian believes he is forbidden to explore.

But what has the Bible to say? It is true that in the Old Testament there is no explicit doctrine of a life to follow death, though there are hints and suggestions; but when we turn to the New Testament, we find that it quickly takes root as one of the cardinal beliefs, and figures in all the Christian creeds—'I believe in the resurrection of the body . . . the life everlasting.' And this hope is based, not upon any experience of the occult, but upon the fact that Jesus Christ himself rose from the dead, and has promised that we too shall share in his resurrection: 'because I live, you shall live also'

(Jn 14:19).

It is important at this stage to distinguish the Christian teaching about life after death from other popular views. The Bible does not simply teach the immortality of the soul. This was the Greek idea, that at death the soul of man was released from his body, rather like a bird from its cage. But the New Testament nowhere suggests that we will be disembodied spirits floating about eternity in a kind of mystified coma. Nor will it have anything to do with what is called 'reincarnation', which is one of the basic beliefs of Hinduism, but is popular in other quarters as well. According to this view, life is a kind of cycle, and we keep reappearing on earth in different forms, our exact place in the batting order in the second innings being determined by our performance in the first. The object is to collect enough merit, or Karma, so that we can attain Moshka, or release from the endless chain of reincarnations, and to be absorbed into Brahma, as a river is absorbed into the sea. Neither Scripture nor experience can adduce a shred of evidence to support this view; nor will Scripture accept another view of life after death which is that we are all merged into some kind of 'world soul', losing our personal identity like a drop of rain in a puddle, or a blackberry in a pot of bramble jelly.

The Christian belief is not based on survival, but resurrection. As we are roused from sleep, so we shall be raised from death, and equipped with an entirely new body adapted to a spiritual world. St Paul goes into this in great detail in that famous fifteenth chapter of First Corinthians, which is frequently read at funerals. He explains that just as you plant a seed and a completely different plant grows up, so while our physical body is buried or cremated, being of no further use to us, God will provide another body, a spiritual one, as different from our present one as perhaps an oak tree is from an acorn.

One of the most fascinating and helpful analogies is also supplied by nature. Take the case of a caterpillar. There comes a time when to all intents and purposes it dies, and becomes a torpid chrysalis. But then the great metamorphosis takes place, and in due course there is raised the moth or butterfly with an entirely different body, perfectly adapted to a completely different environment, no longer earthbound, but airborne; and seeing the earthly body, unless we happened to know, we could have no conception what the heavenly body would be like.

It is idle to speculate what this new, spritual body will be like, and indeed impossible to imagine. I am reminded of the story of the two caterpillars who were deep in conversation with each other when a moth went fluttering past overhead. Looking up, one of the caterpillars said to his friend, 'Ugh! You'll never get me up in one of those things.' He never guessed that it was precisely 'one of those things' that he was destined to become. And it is just about as fruitless an exercise for us to think sensibly of that body which God has prepared for us. What we can be sure about is that it will be as perfectly suited to its environment as our present one is to our life on earth.

From what we read in the New Testament, it seems safe to assume three things. First, we will have *personality*. Just as spirit and body have combined to give us personality in this life, so we can be sure to enjoy the same sort of combination in the next. Heaven will be populated by real people, and Scripture, as we have already seen, has no place in its teaching for the Hindu idea of absorption into some kind of amalgam of souls where we become 'a pulse in the eternal mind'—whatever that may mean.

Secondly, there will be *continuity*. We shall not be a new creation, but the same people that we were before, only differently attired. The things we have done, the lessons we have learnt will be carried over into the next life. No experience need be wasted, and indeed much of what we do and suffer on earth is preparation for the life to come. The word 'Finis' will not be written at the end of the last chapter of our life down here, but 'To be continued'. The next life will not be a new book, but Volume II of the same book.

The third thing we can be sure of is *identity*. It would be unwise to build too much upon the parable of Dives and Lazarus (Lk 16), but in so far as the rich man recognized Lazarus 'afar off', there seems no reason why we shall not be able to do the same with each other. The guise we wear may be different, but the person wearing it will be the same.

It would be a mistake to see in our Lord's resurrection an exact blueprint of our own. He returned to heaven with his human body which suffered no corruption or decay, such as we shall experience when we die. But at the same time we notice that while on earth after his resurrection he possessed the very three things we have just been considering. There was personality, for he walked and talked with the disciples as of old; there was continuity, for they saw his hands and his feet, and he carried through death the marks and experience of his earlier life; and there was identity, for though the disciples were often slow to realize who he was, some familiar word or gesture would betray him, and in the end they would recognize him as the Lord they had known before.

But in what kind of environment will this new body of ours exist and function? Immediately after expressing our belief in 'the resurrection of the body' in the Apostles' Creed, we go on to add the words, 'and the life everlasting'. What does that mean? The notion of everlastingness on its own is not particularly attractive, and we are reminded of the man in the classical legend who asked to be allowed to live for ever, but forgot to ask for perpetual youth, and so went on getting older and older, and more and more isolated. When the Bible speaks of 'everlasting' or 'eternal' life it means something different. It is trying to express the idea of the quality of that life rather than its length. It is different in kind, and not simply in degree—as different, if you like, as the life of the butterfly is from that of the caterpillar it used to be.

'All the world's a stage,' said Shakespeare. I find it helpful sometimes to think of God as an author or a playwright, and his creation as the play. There came a time when he himself, the author, became an actor, and stepped on to the stage and took the part of one of his characters; and then in due course returned to his own world of eternal reality.

When we die, it is as though he beckons to us to step off the stage and join him, and as we do so, we find ourselves in a new world, a world so real that it may even make the old life seem like a dream. The time and space which dictated our stage life are left behind. We are outside their framework, and we find that we can:

> Learn all we lacked before, hear, know and say
> What this tumultuous body now denies;
> And feel, who have laid our groping hands away,
> And see, no longer blinded by our eyes.

Yet how shall we occupy ourselves in the next life? What will we do all day? 'My childhood's conception of heaven was not very attractive,' said that eminent theologian, Dr Charles Raven, 'just sitting on a damp cloud all day harping.' I hope by now he has discovered that there is more to it than that. To begin with, I think we shall find we have new desires and ambitions, and that the kind of things which meant so much to us here on earth will be rather like the toys of our childhood. Marriage, for example, which for most people is perhaps the crowning experience of life, will play no part, according to Jesus, in the hereafter, where 'they neither marry, nor are given in marriage, but are as the angels of God in heaven' (Mt 22:30).

But the Bible makes it plain that there will be plenty of opportunity in heaven for the three main activities of the church militant here on earth— namely fellowship, service and worship. That grand old Victorian hymn of Dean Alford's, once rather irreverently marked on a service sheet as '10,000 × 10,000', sums up this idea of fellowship in words which we would hardly use today, but which come to mean rather more to us as we grow older:

> Oh then what raptured greetings
> On Canaan's happy shore!
> What knittings severed friendships up
> Where partings are no more . . .

We all know the joy of reunions with old friends and members of our family at Christmas and on other special occasions; and this prospect becomes an increasingly attractive one the older we grow, and as more and more of our friends and relations slip over the horizon which we call death.

And if this is one aspect of fellowship, another must surely be the chance we shall have to meet some of those great campaigners of the past, men like Abraham, Moses and Daniel; while to be 'with Christ' (Phil 1:23) in a way which has never been possible before will surely be the crowning experience.

Then we are told that 'his servants shall serve him' (Rev 22:3). Just what form that service will take, we cannot say, but it seems clear from the story Jesus told about the men with their talents (Mt 25:14-30) that we are being prepared here and now for greater responsibility hereafter.

And then there will be worship, and I am using the word in its rather narrower sense of praise and thanksgiving to God. To 'worship' is literally to 'show what someone is worth'. We read of people being given a 'standing ovation', or 'cheered all the way to the wicket'. It is our way of showing what we think they are worth. If we can applaud each other in that way, what about Jesus Christ? We have the answer in the book of Revelation: 'Worthy is the Lamb that was slain to receive power, and riches, and wisdom, and strength, and honour, and glory, and blessing' (Rev 5:12). 'But O eternity's too short to utter all his praise.'

But how on earth are we to think of heaven? Is it a place or a state of mind, a kind of atmosphere, as when we say of some party or excursion, 'It was absolute heaven'? The Bible is quite specific about it. It is a place—the dwelling-place of God, and from the earliest days the Israelites were taught to pray, 'Look down from thy holy habitation, from heaven' (Deut 26:15); while Jesus himself taught us to pray, 'Our Father which art in heaven' (Mt 6:9). But the Bible does not picture God as dwelling there in splendid isolation, for we read of 'heaven . . . with all their host' (Neh 9:6) who worship him there, and Jesus spoke of the 'angels which are in heaven' (Mk 13:32); while Christians too are confidently encouraged to look forward to 'an inheritance . . . reserved in heaven' for them (1 Pet 1:4). Heaven, therefore, is the present abode of God and his angels, and the final destination and home of his people.

When we begin to study the nature of heaven more closely, we are obliged to take refuge in symbols, for this is the only way open to us to describe what is infinitely beyond our present experience and understanding: 'Eye hath not seen, not ear heard, neither have entered into the heart of man, the things which God has prepared for them that love him' (1 Cor 2:9). Moreover, symbols serve as a useful kind of shorthand (e.g. £, @, &, +) which convey the essential meaning of a truth quickly and effectively. And it is in this way, using a kind of symbolic shorthand, that John describes the revelation he received in the last book of the Bible. He wrote it while living as an exile on the island of Patmos in the Aegean. He is thought to have been there from AD 81-96, when he returned to Ephesus under the Emperor Nerva. A grotto is still shown to tourists, where he is thought to have received and recorded his vision.

Although there is much in the book of Revelation that is mysterious and obscure, and scholars are by no means agreed as to its interpretation, a number of the salient facts are clear, even though the language is highly figurative; and we are given some important glimpses of what heaven is like. We are told, for example, that among other things, there will be no sea, no sun and no sin. The Israelites disliked the sea (Rev 21:1). For them the symbol of peace and serenity was the river (Is 48:18; 66:12), while the 'troubled sea', incapable of rest, reminded them of the spiritual turmoil of the wicked (Is 57:20). To them the sea spoke of separation, and its final removal suggested a place where friendships were renewed, and where farewells and partings were no more.

We are told that in the celestial city there will be 'no need of the sun' (Rev 21:23), 'for the glory of God did lighten it and the Lamb is the light thereof'. This is taken to mean that all those things which have brought such glittering pleasure and happiness to us here on earth—all the light we have enjoyed from literature, friendship and nature, for example—will be swallowed up in the glory of God who has given us all these things 'richly . . . to enjoy' (1 Tim 6:17). How brightly these things have shone in this dark world! And how difficult it would have been to have lived without them! But when the day breaks and the sun rises, we shall need them no more. They can be switched off as the street lamps are at dawn, because 'with thee is the fountain of life: in thy light we see light' (Ps 36:9).

No sea and no sun! Perhaps the two things that have brought us most pleasure in life. But it is God's way of telling us that he has 'prepared for us such good things as pass man's understanding', and that we shall not even miss the things we have enjoyed so much on earth:

> O how the city of our God is fair
> If without sea, and sunless though it be,
> For joy of the majestic beauty there,
> Men neither miss the sun, nor mourn the sea.

Lastly, there will be no sin. It is interesting that the Bible begins with a garden from which sin was excluded (Gen 3:24), and now it ends with a city, of which we are told that 'there shall in no wise enter into it anything that defileth, neither whatsover worketh abomination, or maketh a lie' (Rev 21:27). If heaven stands for the presence of God, it also stands for the absence of Satan. The prince of darkness will be finally overthrown, and all his angels with him (Rev 20:10). And it is at this point that the victory won by Christ upon the cross all those years ago will finally be celebrated. At last we shall see all things put under his control (Heb 2:8), and every knee bowed before him (Phil 2:10). He will be all and in all (Col 3:11), and on that day 'The kingdoms of this world are become the kingdoms of our Lord, and of his Christ; and he shall reign for ever and ever' (Rev 11:15).

What has been said so far in this chapter sketches in general outline the Christian teaching about the life which is to come. The Bible doesn't fill in all the details. There is a certain amount of reserve and here and there obscurity, partly due to the fact that it is not always possible to tell whether we are to understand what we read figuratively or literally. For example, it is not clear what will immediately follow death. St Paul's speaks of being 'with Christ' (Phil 1:23) and the dying thief was given the same assurance, that he would be with Christ that very day (Lk 23:42-43). Does that mean that we go straight to heaven, where, as we have seen, Christ is reigning? Because in other places death is spoken of as 'sleep' (1 Thess 4:14) from which we shall be awoken when the time comes. On these matters and on others, Christians agree to differ while sharing the really important conviction 'in the resurrection of the body and the life everlasting'.

We began this book by thinking how each stage of life is in a sense a preparation for the next: the embryo, the child, the adolescent, the adult and the elderly; and now this stage in its turn is one in which we can prepare for the life which is still to come. We have seen a little in this chapter of what that life is all about, and in the next and last chapter we shall consider how we can best prepare ourselves for it.

The Last Enemy

A friendly undertaker in Washington *D.C.* used to close all his correspondence with the words, 'Eventually yours.'

Tide

On Sunday, April 8th, 1945, after holding a short service for his fellow-prisoners, Dietrich Bonhoeffer was led out to the scaffold. As he bade good-bye to the others, he said, 'For me this is the beginning of a new life, eternal life.'

As he lay dying, D.L. Moody awoke from sleep and said, 'Earth recedes. Heaven opens before me. If this is death it is sweet! There is no valley here. God is calling me and I must go.' And a little later he said, 'This is my triumph; this is my coronation day! It is glorious.'

G.W. Ridout

When Sir James Simpson, who discovered anaesthesia, lost his eldest child, he erected on the grave an obelisk pointing skywards. On it were carved the words, 'Nevertheless I live', and above the words a butterfly, to suggest the invincible faith he had in Christ.

We should live our lives as if Christ was coming this afternoon.

Jimmy Carter

For this corruptible must put on incorruption, and this mortal must put on immortality. So when this corruptible shall have put on incorruption, and this mortal shall have put on immortality, then shall be brought to pass the saying that is written, Death is swallowed up in victory. O death, where is thy sting? O grave, where is thy victory? The sting of death is sin; and the strength of sin is the law. But thanks be to God, which giveth us the victory through our Lord Jesus Christ.

1 Cor 15:53-57

10

The Last Enemy

I have often wondered, as I expect everyone has, what my reaction would be if I were told that I was to die tomorrow, peacefully, we will suppose, and painlessly. Dr Johnson tells us that if a man knows he is to die in a fortnight, it 'concentrates his mind wonderfully', everything that needs to be said or done is brought into sharp and vivid focus; but what would be my principal, prevailing emotion? There are I think at least four answers to that question.

Relief

Just now and then we meet people, who, as they put it, 'are longing to go'. It is not that they have not enjoyed life, but everything it held for them has disintegrated and vanished. They are old and infirm, they have outlived all their contemporaries, they are sick and pain-wracked, and they feel they have become an almost unsupportable burden to others. People who have reached that stage can only look upon death as a friend, someone who has come to release them from the bondage of suffering and weakness. As a young man I used rather to shrink from those words in the old Prayer Book funeral service, where we thank God 'that it hath pleased him to deliver this our brother (or sister) out of the miseries of this sinful world', but for the sort of person I have been describing, I can see it makes sense.

In an earlier chapter I wrote of an elderly relation of mine, the only one of her generation who was left in the family. That same evening I heard she had suffered a stroke, and a few days later she died. But as I took part in the funeral service, it was difficult to feel sad. Eighty-nine was not a bad age to have reached, but failing sight, physical weakness and increasing dependence upon others had made life a struggle, and death a quiet and gentle release. Is this what Keats was thinking about when he wrote those haunting words?

> I have been half in love with death
> Called him soft names in many a mused rhyme.

It is difficult, even unnatural, for the young and healthy to realize how death can be, as we say, 'a merciful release'; but for many it is so, and we need to remember that 'death is the cure of all diseases'.

Sorrow

For most of us, however, death is an intrusion. It was never part of God's original plan for his creation, from the very beginning it has been equated with sorrow; and for many, faced with the imminent prospect of death, this would surely be the prevailing emotion, just as it is when those whom we love are taken from us.

This, it would appear, was the frame of mind in which David Watson faced death, and wrote about it in his moving little book, *Fear no Evil*. There was undoubtedly the joy of meeting his Lord face to face and being 'with Christ' for ever; but he admits unashamedly to the distress he felt at leaving his closely-knit family circle. That Jesus felt this sort of sorrow too is obvious from the shortest verse in the Bible where we read that 'Jesus wept' (Jn 11:35); and his tears were not the artificial ones of the hired mourners of those days, but genuine tears of sorrow at the passing of a friend.

But for the Christian sorrow cannot be, must not be, the one surviving emotion. Again and again we are reminded in the New Testament that death is not the end—not a terminus, but a junction; not (as we have already thought) a precipice over which we fall to be seen no more, but a horizon beyond which we pass into a better and a brighter life which God has prepared for us. This is how Paul viewed death, even at the height of his thrillingly adventurous life. It was to be 'with Christ', and that was 'far better' than anything earth could offer him (Phil 1:23).

In the middle ages one of the favourite branches of chemistry was 'Alchemy', the attempt to turn baser metals into gold. In the spiritual sphere men have been pursuing it since time began: how to turn sorrow into joy. They have tried everything— material possessions, intellectual pursuits, aesthetic pleasures, the company of friends; but all to no purpose. Jesus is the only person who can effect that transformation, for he tells us that 'your sorrow shall be turned into joy' (Jn 16:20), because in his presence 'is fulness of joy', and 'at [his] right hand there are pleasures for evermore' (Ps 16:11).

One of the marks of childhood is our close attachment to 'things'. The little boy or girl cannot bear to be parted even for a moment from some piece of rag, or doll, or toy. There is probably some deep psychological reason for this, but although less obviously, and in a more sophisticated manner, this attachment to material things goes with us throughout our lives—the first bicycle, the first car, the first home, and so on. One of the things we have to try to do as we get older is to loosen these material and earthly attachments. It is not an easy thing to do in a world which has sold itself to materialism and consumerism, in which the luxuries of yesterday become the necessities of today and where every day we are confronted with new and attractive objects which are so designed to make life easier, happier and more comfortable. It is for this reason that I have always been rather frightened of becoming a collector of any one thing—pictures, antiques, even stamps. In my case it would be rather like planting ivy; sooner or later it would begin to grip and throttle the thing it was merely intended to decorate.

I remember my father writing to me towards the end of his life and saying that as he grew older ideas had begun to mean more to him than things, and it was in such concepts as truth, beauty and goodness that he found increasing satisfaction. I think I am beginning to see what he meant, for I find I no longer want to possess things simply for their own sake, but rather for the purpose which they serve. When we are young, the acquisitive spirit is very strong. We feel we can only enjoy something if we possess it. As we get older, this should begin to disappear, and we find we can enjoy what others possess without any desire to acquire it for ourselves. A landowner was once displaying his property to a friend, and sweeping his arm he said, 'As far as you can see, the land is mine.' 'Yes,' was the quiet reply, 'but the landscape is mine.' I think that is what Jesus must have meant when he said that 'the meek . . . shall inherit the earth' (Mt 5:5). They don't conquer it, or purchase it, or possess it; but in a very real sense it is theirs. And I believe it is towards this paradox of 'having nothing, and yet possessing all things' (2 Cor 6:10) that the elderly Christian must strive.

I write tentatively about all this, and not as one who has already attained. I know only too well how grieved I would be if fire or theft robbed me of some of my earthly treasures, though people who have suffered in this way often seem to be lightened rather than burdened by the experience. But if as life goes on we can loosen the ropes which bind us so firmly to this world, it will make the final parting, when it comes, much less painful and traumatic.

I often ponder those words which were spoken in the parable to 'the rich fool' (Lk 12:20): 'Thou fool, this night, thy soul shall be required of thee . . .' This wealthy and successful farmer made three mistakes. He thought his careful, materialistic plans for the future were wise; but he was really a *fool*. He thought he had plenty of time; but he was summoned that *night*. He provided for his body, but God was interested in his *soul*. He was not ready

for the unexpected 'lift-off'. He was 'overweight'.
How different was St Paul! 'I am now ready to be
offered, and the time of my departure is at hand
. . .' (2 Tim 4:6).

Fear

The third emotion which people experience in the
face of death is fear. This again is natural. Death is
spoken of in the Bible as 'the last enemy' (1 Cor
15:26). You expect to meet your strongest op-
ponent in the final, and that is where we meet
death. There is something so conclusive, so irreversible, so inescapable about death that it does
strike a chill at the heart of all normal people.

I have never ceased to admire, as one who is
conscious of conspicuously lacking it himself, the
courage with which men and women are sometimes prepared to hazard their lives. Quite recently
I watched again that film of the Israeli raid on
Entebbe Airport, and marvelled at the seeming indifference of those men to danger and death.
True, such people usually tell us that they certainly
do know the meaning of fear, but they seem to
have an almost miraculous way of disguising the
fact.

But need the Christian be afraid of death? It is
true that he may share the average person's horror
of dying, and the pain and weakness which often
accompany it; but need he fear what lies beyond
the grave? As that lovely Easter hymn puts it, 'Jesus
lives! thy terrors now can O death no more appal
us'. Jesus has met, fought and conquered that 'last
enemy'. He has removed the sting of death, ren-
dering it harmless. He has defused it, as a time

bomb might be defused, so that it need never explode in our faces. He has destroyed the substance of death, and left only its shadow, and while a shadow may hide us for a time, it can neither hurt not harm us.

There is a lovely and important verse in the epistle to the Hebrews where we are told that Jesus, 'by the grace of God should taste death for every man' (Heb 2:9). The primary meaning has to do with his sacrificial death upon the cross, and the fact that because of it we are 'ransomed, healed, restored, forgiven'. But there is also a secondary meaning which St Chrysostom refers to, namely that on behalf of all of us he sampled death, demonstrated the fact that it was not the fatal thing it seemed to be and proved it by rising from the dead. Perhaps you can remember as a child making a tremendous fuss over some medicine which your mother or nurse was trying to persuade you to take. Finally, in a desperate attempt to allay your fears, she took a tiny sip of it herself. Her survival and her smiling face finally convinced you that it could not be as bad as you feared, and closing your eyes and holding your nose you gulped it down. There was after all no poison in the cup, and you came triumphantly through the ordeal.

The Christian knows too that he is not asked to go through that long, dark tunnel alone. 'Yea, though I walk through the valley of the shadow of death, I will fear no evil: for thou art with me; thy rod and thy staff they comfort me' (Ps 23:4). Peace of mind in a crisis is not the absence of danger, but the presence of Christ. You don't sweeten the coffee by extracting something from the beans, but by adding sugar to the cup.

The country town where I live, Crowborough, in East Sussex, had its moment of glory in World War II. There lived here at that time a school teacher named Minnie Louise Haskins (1875–1957). Overnight she became famous, because King George VI, in his first Christmas broadcast of the war, quoted some words she had written, and which now appear on the memorial window to him in the Queen's Chapel of the Savoy. 'I said to the man who stood at the gate of the year, "Give me a light that I may step safely into the unknown." But he said to me, "Go forth into the darkness, and put your hand into the hand of God. That shall be to you better than light, and safer than a known way."'

It is with words like these that our Lord greets the Christian pilgrim towards the end of his journey. We need no reassuring voices from the other side, no mediums or occult experiences. It is enough for us that Christ died and rose again, and is able to turn to us and say, 'I am he that liveth and was dead; and, behold, I am alive for evermore' (Rev 1:18). It follows therefore that the more closely to Christ we can live during our earthly lives, the easier and the more natural it will be for us to pass through death into his immediate presence. As the hymn puts it, 'Fear him, you saints, and you will then have nothing else to fear.'

But what are we to say about those who have rejected Christ while they have been down here on earth, and found no place for him in their lives? Have they nothing to fear? No faithful treatment of this subject can ignore or minimize the many warnings contained in Scripture concerning those who, having been given the opportunity of yielding their lives to Christ, have deliberately turned their backs upon him. They are described by St Paul as 'having no hope, and without God' (Eph 2:12); and the writer to the Hebrews reminds us that 'It is a fearful thing to fall into the hands of the living God' (Heb 10:31).

We are treading very serious and solemn ground here, but there seems to be no escape from the stark teaching of the New Testament on this subject, namely that man's eternal destiny is settled in this life according to his response to the claims of Christ (Jn 3:36). If there are any who have read thus far in this book, and find themselves answering to this description, then the glorious news is still true, that Christ died to bring forgiveness, and that all who turn to him in penitence and faith may find it in their own personal experience. Age is no barrier either way.

The youngest child can put its trust in Jesus, and I have met many grown-ups who date their commitment to him to a time when they were seven or eight, or even younger. At the same time he is waiting to receive someone who may have ignored him for seventy or eighty years. Nor should such people be deterred by a wasted or even wicked life. Even in the Nuremberg prison there were Nazi war criminals who found peace in Christ at the last, for 'the vilest offender who truly believes that moment from Jesus a pardon receives'.

Shame

There is a fourth emotion which some feel at the approach of death, and that is shame—the sense that they might have done so much more for their

Master while here on earth, and have so little to show him by way of gratitude for all that he has done for them. They are like the builder described by St Paul (1 Cor 3) who started with a solid, stone foundation, but instead of using lasting materials, used wood, hay and straw. The fire destroyed it, and at the end he had nothing to show except the beginning. Or again, Jesus told a story to illustrate much the same truth. Three men were given money to trade with. Two used it wisely and made a solid capital gain. The third simply buried his in the ground (Mt 25:14-30).

Several times in the New Testament we are exhorted to be 'stirred up'. For example, St Paul writing to Timothy says, 'Stir up the gift of God, which is in thee' (2 Tim 1:6). I remember once being given a cup of coffee with which I always prefer sugar, but seeing none about, and not liking to trouble my host, I drank it as it was. As I finished it, I found to my dismay at the bottom of the cup a little soggy puddle of brown sugar which had been there all the time, but unstirred. How sad and shaming to come to the end of our life and find that that had happened! A saved soul, but a wasted life.

In 2 Timothy 2:15 St Paul speaks of two kinds of 'workmen', those who are 'approved' and those who are 'ashamed'. It is easy in old age to grow slack, to think that we have 'done our bit', to start free-wheeling, and to suppose that nothing very strenuous or demanding is expected of us. If we are tempted to think like that, we need to remember Abraham, Moses, Daniel and Paul himself. How ashamed they would have felt if they had failed to respond to the call that came to them in old age! As it was they lived to serve God in outstanding ways, and but for their devoted and fruitful retirement, we might never have heard of them.

I had an interesting experience recently. I attended a reunion party of a number of men who had come up to Cambridge with me as undergraduates before the war. Some of them I had not seen for nearly fifty years and some I would not have recognized without the labels they were wearing. I kept saying to myself, 'Who are all these old men?', forgetting that they were thinking exactly the same about me. We had all changed. Some were bald and some grey; some seemed to have put on weight and others lost it; some seemed bigger than I remembered them to be, and some smaller. We all appeared to have changed in different ways.

And just as the years bring an inevitable outward change, so they should bring an inward, spiritual change, but in one direction only, namely in an increasing likeness to our Lord and Master Jesus Christ (2 Cor 3:18). The Christian is someone who has been 'transferred' (Col 1:13, Revised Standard Version) that he may be 'transformed' (Rom 12:2). The 'transferring' is a crisis, but the 'transforming' a lifelong process.

We might compare the Christian to a Frenchman who becomes naturalized as an Englishman. There is one moment when he was a Frenchman and another when he became an Englishman; but becoming truly English is a long, slow and perhaps painful process, and to the very end of his life there will still be traces and vestigial remains, though decreasingly few, of his French origins.

So it is possible to be a Christian without being

Christlike (just as it is possible to be a man without being manly, or a lady without being lady-like). But it is God's purpose for all his children that they should grow in likeness to his Son, Jesus Christ (1 Jn 3:2). Going back to the reunion I attended, however hard we found it to recognize each other, and however much we had changed from the fresh-faced undergraduates of 1935, there ought to have been one direction in which we had all developed and which made us instantly recognizable to God: our likeness to his Son—the family likeness.

The French artist, Gustave Doré (1832-83) was once travelling into Italy, but he found on reaching the frontier that he had mislaid his passport. A protracted argument followed, until finally the officials gave him permission to prove his identity by drawing for them a picture of their king, Victor Emmanuel. He called for paper and pencil, and with a few deft strokes drew a perfect likeness of the king, and on the strength of that, he was allowed to cross the frontier. Of course it will not be quite like that with us. Our acceptance into heaven depends upon what Christ has done for us, and not what we have done for him. But St Peter in one place says, 'give diligence to make your calling and election sure. . . . For so an entrance shall be ministered unto you abundantly into the everlasting kingdom of our Lord and Saviour Jesus Christ' (2 Pet 1:10-11). This seems to imply that although all who trust in Christ will be received into heaven, some will receive a more abundant welcome than others. It is as though some will be instantly recognized, and others will have to be looked up in the register; and the test will be their likeness to Christ.

So, to the very end we need to cultivate our own

spiritual lives. We never reach a point, however old, experienced and revered we may grow, when we can say, 'I have arrived.' To the very end we shall be learners, and can never remove the letter 'L' from our lives, and be trusted out alone. We must so live that 'when he shall appear, we may have confidence, and not be ashamed before him at his coming' (1 Jn 2:28).

'At his coming.' We must never forget that we may not actually live to see death, because Christ may return while we are still alive. It is curious that a doctrine, so prominent in the New Testament, is so seldom preached about from the pulpits of our churches. Again and again he referred to his personal return, and it was the constant theme of his disciples and apostles; and at the very moment of departure they were told that 'this same Jesus, which is taken up from you into heaven, shall so come in like manner as you have seen him go into heaven' (Acts 1:11). How do we account for this conspiracy of silence?

First, it is a doctrine which is doubted, even by some Christians. Nearly two thousand years have gone by, and still it seems to be no nearer than in the days when the apostles seemed to be expecting it almost daily. We were warned that this would be so, and that there would come a time when people would say, 'Where is the promise of his coming?' (2 Pet 3:4). But we need to remember that time means nothing with God, in whose eyes a thousand years are like a single day, and vice versa (2 Pet 3:8). Have you sometimes had a dream, spanning perhaps days and even weeks, and then woken up to discover that you have been asleep for no more than a few minutes? Time is measured differently in the dream world from the way it is in the real world; and I sometimes think it is like that with us and God.

Secondly, this doctrine is often distorted. Foolish people, with no authority for doing so, have tried to foretell the exact time and circumstances of Christ's return, and this has brought the truth itself into cynical disrepute. I can still remember one such attempt. The date fixed was May 29th, 1929. It was a Wednesday, and I seem to remember there was a school cricket match in which I was due to play. Happily to my childish mind the match took place as arranged. Why people feel they have to indulge this sort of forecasting has always puzzled me, because we are specifically told that the day of his return is known only to God, and that Jesus will come like a thief in the night (Lk 12:39-40); and whoever heard of a thief advertising in advance the day of his arrival? In other words, the very fact that people think they can fix a date proves them to be wrong.

Thirdly, the doctrine of the second coming of Christ is disturbing. It certainly ought not to be for Christians, who should be anxious to welcome Christ; but for those who have rejected him, it must understandably cause alarm and concern. On another May day—May 25th, 1660, Charles Stuart returned to this country as Charles II. For many, indeed for most people, it was a day of tremendous joy, and he was rapturously received, first on the coast and then again in London. But for others—those who had been disloyal, or who had plotted against him, or even been half-hearted in their allegiance—it must have been a very disturbing time, and we can imagine that they must have been 'ashamed at his coming', and anxious to keep out of his way.

We have compared retirement to a 'mini-death', but it would be equally true to make the comparison the other way round, and say that death itself is like a mini-retirement. Paul tells us that our true citizenship is in heaven (Phil 3:20, New International Version) and the writer to the Hebrews tells us that down here on earth we have no permanent home (Heb 13:14), but are rather like British citizens living and working abroad, in some distant part of the world. When the time comes for us to die, we 'retire' to the homeland which is heaven, for that is where we really belong. That is where our future lies, and that is where, if we are wise, our treasure has been invested (Mt 6:19-21). It follows that the older we get, the more our eyes should be turned in that direction, the more we should prepare ourselves for our eventual 'return', and the more 'our hearts should surely there be fixed where true joys are to be found'.

With the coming of old age, people find that the old earthly ambitions which have motivated them begin to fade away. The competition in life is over. The 'rat-race', if we have been involved in it, is a thing of the past; and even those who have reached the very top find that retirement and old age are great levellers. The famous politician becomes a private citizen, even if he is given a peerage, the bishop sheds the legal trappings of his office, the general his uniform, and the judge and headmaster lay down their authority and become like other men.

But for the Christian there remains one ambition which must motivate him to the very end— that he will be worthy of an abundant welcome when finally he reaches the shores of his homeland, and that he will not feel himself to be a stranger and out of place in the company he finds there. It was this that dominated the thinking of the aged apostle Paul (Phil 3:10-14). You might think that at this age he had arrived, but this is not how he saw it, for like an ambitious climber, there was always one more peak to be conquered.

It is one of the paradoxes of the Christian life that 'they who fain would serve him best are conscious most of wrong within'. In his early days Paul said that he was 'not fit to be called an apostle' (1 Cor 15:9 New English Bible). A few years later, after growing steadily as a Christian, he rated himself still lower, as 'less than the least of all saints' (Eph 3:8); while towards the very end of his life, when everyone else regarded him as a spiritual giant, he referred to himself as 'the foremost of sinners' (1 Tim 1.15, Revised Standard Version). We find an echo of this paradox in one of the hymns of F.W. Faber:

> I often feel in my own thoughts
> When they lie nearest thee,
> That the worst man I have ever met
> Was a better man than me.

It is probably true of most disciplines that 'the more you know, the more you know you don't know', and no doubt most scientists, historians and others would subscribe to that maxim. It is certainly true in Christian experience, and explains why Paul's one ambition, after years of Christian progress was, *That I may know him . . .* ' (Phil 3:10).

Jesus said, 'this is life eternal, that they might

know thee the only true God, and Jesus Christ, whom thou hast sent' (Jn 17:3). 'Life,' said Herbert Spencer, is the ability to correspond with your environment.' A stone is dead, because it can make no such response, but a tree, on the other hand, has life, because it reacts to light, heat and humidity. Moving up the scale, we can say that a dog has more advanced life, because its reactions are altogether sharper and wider; while human beings enjoy higher life still, because there is a whole world of art, music, science, literature and so on which is closed to even the most advanced animals, but is part of our everyday heritage. But is that as far as we can go? Not according to Jesus; for he tells us that eternal, spiritual life belongs to those who have responded to him and entered into a personal relationship with him.

But eternal life is not something we wait to receive when we die. It can begin here and now, the moment we put our trust in Christ, and will continue hereafter. This knowledge of Christ, this relationship with him, will transcend death, and will be quite unaffected by it. It will follow us out of time and into eternity. For after all, what is time, but the suburb of eternity, and death the bridge that leads from the one to the other?